Introduction to R for Business Intelligence

Learn how to leverage the power of R for Business Intelligence

Jay Gendron

BIRMINGHAM - MUMBAI

Introduction to R for Business Intelligence

First published: August 2016

Production reference: 1230816

Published by Packt Publishing Ltd.
Livery Place
35 Livery Street
Birmingham
B3 2PB, UK.
ISBN 978-1-78528-025-2

www.packtpub.com

Credits

Author
Jay Gendron

Reviewers
Fabien Richard
Jeffrey Strickland, Ph.D.

Commissioning Editor
Veena Pagare

Acquisition Editors
Usha Iyer
Manish Nainani

Content Development Editor
Siddhesh Salvi

Technical Editor
Pranil Pathare

Copy Editor
Vibha Shukla

Project Coordinator
Nidhi Joshi

Proofreader
Safis Editing

Indexer
Aishwarya Gangawane

Graphics
Disha Haria

Production Coordinator
Nilesh Mohite

About the Author

Jay Gendron is an associate data scientist working with Booz Allen Hamilton. He has worked in the fields of machine learning, data analysis, and statistics for over a decade, and believes that good questions and compelling visualization make analytics accessible to decision makers. Jay is a business leader, entrepreneurial employee, artist, and author. He has a B.S.M.E. in mechanical engineering, an M.S. in management of technology, an M.S. in operations research, and graduate certificates for chief information officer and IT program management.

Jay is a lifelong learner—a member of the first cohort to earn the 10-course specialization in data science by Johns Hopkins University on Coursera. He is an award-winning speaker who has presented internationally and provides *pro bono* data science expertise to numerous not-for-profit organizations to improve their operational insights. Connect with Jay Gendron at `https://www.linkedin.com/in/jaygendron`, visit `http://jgendron.github.io/`, or Twitter `@jaygendron`.

Acknowledgement

I am most grateful to *God*. He has given all of us individual gifts so that we can serve others in this life. I am thankful for the opportunities and abilities that He has bestowed upon me.

I wish to express heartfelt love and gratitude to my wife, *Cindy*. She is my toughest critic and my greatest coach. She has been with me during every step of this journey. She was there during the toughest of times and celebrated the book's completion. This book would not exist without her loving support. For that, I thank her more than mere words can express.

Thank you to section contributor, *Shantanu Saha*. He is a talented and energetic data scientist. Shantanu contributed his skills to help author *Chapter 7, Visualizing the Data's Story*. He has a great future in this field and I look forward to seeing his work as he continues to analyze and write.

I would like to also thank the author of the BI Tips, *Jesse Barboza*, who has developed business intelligence systems for over 12 years. One goal of this book was to enhance cross-functional understanding between the analytic and business communities. Jesse created tips for both, R developers new to the business and business analysts new to R.

Finally, I would like to thank the contributing authors, *Rick Jones* (*Chapter 4, Linear Regression for Business*) and *Steven Mortimer* (*Chapter 8, Web Dashboards with Shiny*). Steven was also a major contributor to *Chapter 7, Visualizing the Data's Story*. Their perspectives bring better insights and greater value to the book.

Contributing Authors:

Rick Jones

I would like to thank Rick Jones for his work in developing the statistical approaches and rigor in *Chapter 4, Linear Regression for Business*. Rick is a retired United States Navy SEAL officer. While on active duty, he was awarded a subspecialty in information technology management for having spent over six years managing IT research, development, and acquisition programs. He also worked as a computer scientist at the United States Naval Research Laboratory, where he led the development of a wireless network emulator to function as the testbed in a Defense Advanced Research Projects Agency cybersecurity program. After ten years in systems development as a civilian, Rick made a career shift to data analytics, where he has been active in developing a data science community in Norfolk, Virginia. He currently works as a data science consultant and specializes in machine learning classification problems. He has master's degrees in information systems technology and applied statistics.

Steven Mortimer

Steven Mortimer has provided readers great insights by authoring *Chapter 8, Web Dashboards with Shiny*. The app design and thought process is immensely useful in a web-based world relying more on data products. Steven is a statistician-turned-data scientist. His passion for helping others make data-driven decisions has led to a variety of projects in the healthcare, higher education, and dot-com industries. The constant in his experiences has been utilizing the R ecosystem of tools, including RStudio, R Markdown, and Shiny. He is an active contributor to a few R packages, acting as a contributor to the `RForcecom` package and author and creator of the `rdfp` and `roas` packages. Steven holds a master's degree in statistics from the University of Virginia. Much of his code is publicly available in his GitHub repositories at `https://github.com/ReportMort`.

Kannan Kalidasan

Kannan Kalidasan, a data engineer at Expedia Inc., is an autodidact and an open source evangelist.

He has 10 years of work experience in data management, distributed computing, and analytics, contributing as a developer, architect, tech lead, and DBA.

He was one of the technical reviewers for the book *R Data Visualization Cookbook* published by *Packt Publishing*.

He, being passionate about technology, had his own tech startup in 2005, when he was pursuing his bachelor of technology (computer science) from Pondicherry University.

He loves to mentor fellow enthusiasts, take long walks alone, write poems in Tamil, paint, and read books. He blogs at `https://kannandreams.wordpress.com/` and tweets at `@kannanpoem`.

> *Big thanks to all those who have been a great support and believed that I could do something substantial in life.*

About the Reviewers

Fabien Richard has a master's degree in computer science engineering from Polytech Nantes, France. He is currently a software engineer and data specialist at a leading company for real-time telecom market data and consumer behavior analytics in North America. He applies business intelligence methods and parallel processing techniques to build fast, reliable, and scalable data processes. Since he started learning to code, Fabien has been driven by the pleasure of helping the sports and school communities around him through the development of web applications. His project about the energy consumption of the Internet won the first prize in the Hyblab data journalism competition in 2014. Fabien is also interested in business management, and more specifically how to leverage data to drive business decisions and create monetizable knowledge.

Jeffrey Strickland, Ph.D., is the author of *Data Analytics using Open-Source Tools, Lulu.com* and a Senior Analytics Scientist with Clarity Solution Group. He has performed predictive modeling, simulation, and analysis for the Department of Defense, NASA, the Missile Defense Agency, and the Financial and Insurance Industries for over 20 years. Jeffrey is a Certified Modeling and Simulation Professional (CMSP) and an Associate Systems Engineering Professional (ASEP). He has published nearly 200 blogs on LinkedIn, is also a frequently invited guest speaker and the author of 20 books including:

- *Operations Research using OpenSource Tools*
- *Discrete Event Simulation Using ExtendSim 8*
- *Introduction to Crime Analysis and Mapping*
- *Missile Flight Simulation*
- *Mathematical Modeling of Warfare and Combat Phenomenon*
- *Predictive Modeling and Analytics*
- *Using Math to Defeat the Enemy: Combat Modeling for Simulation*
- *Verification and Validation for Modeling and Simulation*
- *Simulation Conceptual Modeling*
- *Systems Engineering Processes and Practice*

Connect with Jeffrey Strickland at https://www.linkedin.com/in/jeffreystrickland.

www.PacktPub.com

eBooks, discount offers, and more

Did you know that Packt offers eBook versions of every book published, with PDF and ePub files available? You can upgrade to the eBook version at www.PacktPub.com and as a print book customer, you are entitled to a discount on the eBook copy. Get in touch with us at customercare@packtpub.com for more details.

At www.PacktPub.com, you can also read a collection of free technical articles, sign up for a range of free newsletters and receive exclusive discounts and offers on Packt books and eBooks.

https://www2.packtpub.com/books/subscription/packtlib

Do you need instant solutions to your IT questions? PacktLib is Packt's online digital book library. Here, you can search, access, and read Packt's entire library of books.

Why subscribe?

- Fully searchable across every book published by Packt
- Copy and paste, print, and bookmark content
- On demand and accessible via a web browser

Table of Contents

Preface

"*Most organizations early on in the data-science learning curve spend most of their time assembling data and not analyzing it. Mature data science organizations realize that in order to be successful they must enable their members to access and use all available data—not some of the data, not a subset, not a sample, but all data. A lawyer wouldn't go to court with only some of the evidence to support their case—they would go with all appropriate evidence. ...The fundamental building block of a successful and mature data science capability is the ability to ask the right types of questions of the data. This is rooted in the understanding of how the business runs... The mature data science organization has a collaborative culture in which the data science team works side by side with the business to solve critical problems using data. ... [it] includes one or more people with the skills of a data artist and a data storyteller. Stories and visualizations are where we make connections between facts. They enable the listener to understand better the context (What?), the why (So what?), and "what will work" in the future (Now what?).*"*
 - Peter Guerra and Kirk Borne in Ten Signs of Data Science Maturity (2016)*

Guerra and *Borne* (2016) highlight the importance of a diverse and inquisitive team approach to data science. Business intelligence also benefits from this approach. *Introduction to R for Business Intelligence* gives you a way to explore the world of business intelligence through the eyes of an analyst working in a successful and growing startup company. You will learn R through use cases supporting different business functions.

This book provides data-driven and analytically focused approaches to help you answer business questions in operations, marketing, and finance—a diverse perspective. You will also see how asking the right type of questions and developing the stories and visualizations helps you connect the dots between the data and the business.

Enjoy the journey as you code solutions to business intelligence problems using R.
- Jay Gendron

What this book covers

This book is written in three parts that represent a natural flow in the data science process: data preparation, analysis, and presentation of results.

In *Part 1*, you will learn about extracting data from different sources and cleaning that data.

Chapter 1, *Extract, Transform, and Load*, begins your journey with the ETL process by extracting data from multiple sources, transforming the data to fit analysis plans, and loading the transformed data into business systems for analysis.

Chapter 2, *Data Cleaning*, leads you through a four-step cleaning process applicable to many types of datasets. You will learn how to summarize, fix, convert, and adapt data in preparation for your analysis process.

In *Part 2*, you will look at data exploration, predictive models, and cluster analysis for business intelligence, as well as how to forecast time series data.

Chapter 3, *Exploratory Data Analysis*, continues the adventure by exploring an unfamiliar dataset using a structured approach. This will provide you insights about features important for shaping further analysis.

Chapter 4, *Linear Regression for Business*, (co-authored with *Rick Jones*) walks you through a classic predictive analysis approach for single and multiple features. It also reinforces key assumptions the data should meet in order to use this analytic technique.

Chapter 5, *Data Mining with Cluster Analysis*, presents two methods of unsupervised learning with examples using k-means and hierarchical clustering. These two data mining techniques allow you to unearth patterns hidden in the data.

Chapter 6, *Time Series Analysis*, introduces a difficult topic not often taught in data science courses. You will explore non-machine learning methods to forecast future values with data that are dependent on past observations.

Finally, in *Part 3* you will learn to communicate results with sharp visualizations and interactive, web-based dashboards.

Chapter 7, *Visualizing the Data's Story*, explores more than just techniques to interactively visualize your results. You will learn how your audience cognitively interprets data through color, shape, and position.

Chapter 8, *Web Dashboards with Shiny*, (authored by *Steven Mortimer*) culminates your adventure by explaining how to create a web-based, business intelligence application using R Shiny.

There are a number of appendices providing additional information and code.

Appendix A, *References*, provides a list of the references used throughout the book.

Appendix B, *Other Helpful R Functions*, provides a list of functions and their descriptions. These are useful in data science projects and this appendix allows you to explore how they may help you work with data.

Appendix C, *R Packages Used in the Book*, gives a complete list of all the R packages used in each chapter. This allows you to install all the packages you will need by referring to a single list. It also contains instructions on installing packages.

Appendix D, *R Code for Supporting Market Segment Business Case Calculations*, gives a detailed code base for computing the geo-based information used in *Chapter 5, Data Mining with Cluster Analysis*.

After completing the use cases, you will be able to work with business data in the R programming environment and realize how data science helps make informed decisions when developing business strategy. Along the way, you will find helpful tips about R and business intelligence.

What you need for this book

You need the R statistical package, available free as an open source download from CRAN (https://www.r-project.org/). This book used R version 3.3.1 for Windows. You will get the same results using the macOS or Linux software.

Optionally, it is also recommended that you use RStudio Desktop, an open source user interface that works with R (https://www.rstudio.com/). This book used version 0.99.903 for Windows. It is also available for macOS and Linux.

Lastly, you will need to install a variety of R packages to perform the various analyses. All these are all freely available using the install.packages() function within R. You can get a refresher on installing packages in Appendix C, *R Packages Used in the Book*.

This book provides code using the R statistical programming language. Perhaps it has been a while since you last used or learned R. If that is the case, then you may find the following material quite useful. It provides a listing of R skills that you should know before working on the use cases provided in each of the chapters.

Video links (*Peng, 2015; Peng, 2014; LawrenceStats, 2016; Peng, 2012*) for each skill provide an explanation of techniques that you may want to review before continuing:

Skill	Chapter	Video resource
Installing R	1	Windows: `https://www.youtube.com/watch?v=Ohnk9hcxf9M` macOS: `https://www.youtube.com/watch?v=uxuuWXU-7UQ`
Installing R Studio	1	Windows and macOS: `https://www.youtube.com/watch?v=bM7Sfz-LADM;feature=youtu.be;t=1s`
Installing R packages	1	`https://www.youtube.com/watch?v=H3EFjKngPr4`
Setting working directory	1	Windows: `https://www.youtube.com/watch?v=XBcvH1BpIBo` macOS: `https://www.youtube.com/watch?v=8xT3hmJQskU`
Data types	1	Part 1: `https://www.youtube.com/watch?v=vGY5i_J2c-c` Part 2: `https://www.youtube.com/watch?v=w8_XdYI3reU` Part 3: `https://www.youtube.com/watch?v=NuY6jY4qE7I`
Basic scripting	1	Control structures (part 1): `https://www.youtube.com/watch?v=8RmwEBo8yy` Control structures (part 2): `https://www.youtube.com/watch?v=z8V-a6d8JTg`
Basic plotting	2	Base plotting (part 1): `https://www.youtube.com/watch?v=AAXhegb5WM` Base plotting (part 2): `https://www.youtube.com/watch?v=bhyb1gCeAVk`
Subsetting data	2	Subsetting basics: `https://www.youtube.com/watch?v=VfZUZGUgHqg` Subsetting matrices: `https://www.youtube.com/watch?v=FzjXesh9tRw`

Who this book is for

This book is for business analysts who want to increase their skills in R and learn analytic approaches to business problems. Data science professionals will benefit from this book as they apply their R skills to business problems and learn the language of business.

Conventions

In this book, you will find a number of text styles that distinguish between different kinds of information. Here are some examples of these styles and an explanation of their meaning.

Code words in text, database table names, folder names, filenames, file extensions, pathnames, dummy URLs, user input, and Twitter handles are shown as follows: "You can load the Bike Sharing data file into the R environment by using the read.csv() function."

A block of code is set as follows:

```
bike$holiday <- factor(bike$holiday, levels = c(0, 1),
                       labels = c("no", "yes"))
bike$workingday <- factor(bike$workingday, levels = c(0, 1),
                          labels = c("no", "yes"))
```

When we wish to draw your attention to a particular part of a code block, the relevant lines or items are set in bold:

```
query <- "SELECT * FROM marketing"
bike <- sqlQuery(connection, query)
close(connection)
```

Any command-line input or output is written as follows:

```
[1] TRUE
```

New terms and **important words** are shown in bold. Words that you see on the screen, for example, in menus or dialog boxes, appear in the text like this: "RStudio will automatically create a `ui.R` and `server.R` file, if you create a new project and choose **New Directory** and **Shiny Web Application** as the type."

Warnings or important notes appear in a box like this.

Tips and tricks appear like this.

Reader feedback

Feedback from our readers is always welcome. Let us know what you think about this book-what you liked or disliked. Reader feedback is important for us as it helps us develop titles that you will really get the most out of. To send us general feedback, simply e-mail `feedback@packtpub.com`, and mention the book's title in the subject of your message. If there is a topic that you have expertise in and you are interested in either writing or contributing to a book, see our author guide at `www.packtpub.com/authors`.

Customer support

Now that you are the proud owner of a Packt book, we have a number of things to help you to get the most from your purchase.

Downloading the example code

You can download the example code files for this book from your account at `http://www.packtpub.com`. If you purchased this book elsewhere, you can visit `http://www.packtpub.com/support` and register to have the files e-mailed directly to you.

You can download the code files by following these steps:

1. Log in or register to our website using your e-mail address and password.
2. Hover the mouse pointer on the **SUPPORT** tab at the top.
3. Click on **Code Downloads & Errata**.

4. Enter the name of the book in the **Search** box.
5. Select the book for which you're looking to download the code files.
6. Choose from the drop-down menu where you purchased this book from.
7. Click on **Code Download**.

Once the file is downloaded, please make sure that you unzip or extract the folder using the latest version of:

- WinRAR / 7-Zip for Windows
- Zipeg / iZip / UnRarX for Mac
- 7-Zip / PeaZip for Linux

The code bundle for the book is also hosted on GitHub at https://github.com/PacktPublishing/Introduction-To-R-For-Business-Intelligence. We also have other code bundles from our rich catalog of books and videos available at https://github.com/PacktPublishing/. Check them out!

Downloading the color images of this book

We also provide you with a PDF file that has color images of the screenshots/diagrams used in this book. The color images will help you better understand the changes in the output. You can download this file from https://www.packtpub.com/sites/default/files/downloads/IntroductionToRForBusinessIntelligence_ColorImages.pdf.

Errata

Although we have taken every care to ensure the accuracy of our content, mistakes do happen. If you find a mistake in one of our books-maybe a mistake in the text or the code-we would be grateful if you could report this to us. By doing so, you can save other readers from frustration and help us improve subsequent versions of this book. If you find any errata, please report them by visiting http://www.packtpub.com/submit-errata, selecting your book, clicking on the **Errata Submission Form** link, and entering the details of your errata. Once your errata are verified, your submission will be accepted and the errata will be uploaded to our website or added to any list of existing errata under the **Errata** section of that title.

To view the previously submitted errata, go to https://www.packtpub.com/books/content/support and enter the name of the book in the search field. The required information will appear under the **Errata** section.

Piracy

Piracy of copyrighted material on the Internet is an ongoing problem across all media. At Packt, we take the protection of our copyright and licenses very seriously. If you come across any illegal copies of our works in any form on the Internet, please provide us with the location address or website name immediately so that we can pursue a remedy.

Please contact us at `copyright@packtpub.com` with a link to the suspected pirated material.

We appreciate your help in protecting our authors and our ability to bring you valuable content.

Questions

If you have a problem with any aspect of this book, you can contact us at `questions@packtpub.com`, and we will do our best to address the problem.

1
Extract, Transform, and Load

Business may focus on profits and sales, but **business intelligence (BI)** focuses on data. Activities reliant on data require the business analyst to acquire it from diverse sources. The term **Extract, Transform, and Load**, commonly referred to as **ETL**, is a deliberate process to get, manipulate, and store data to meet business or analytic needs. ETL is the starting point for many business analytic projects. Poorly executed ETL may affect a business in the form of added cost and lost time to make decisions. This chapter covers the following four key topics:

- Understanding big data in BI analytics
- Extracting data from sources
- Transforming data to fit analytic needs
- Loading data into business systems for analysis

This chapter presents each ETL step within the context of the R computational environment. Each step is broken down into finer levels of detail and includes a variety of situations that business analysts encounter when executing BI in a big data business world.

Understanding big data in BI analytics

Before we begin describing the ETL process, consider its importance in business intelligence. *CIO Magazine* provides a popular and useful definition of BI (*Mulcahy, 2007*):

> *"Business intelligence, or BI, is an umbrella term that refers to a variety of software applications used to analyze an organization's raw data. BI as a discipline is made up of several related activities, including data mining, online analytical processing, querying and reporting."*

Mulcahy captures the essence of this book, which presents solutions in R to walk you through the steps from data analytic techniques to communicating your results. The purpose of BI applications has changed over the last decade as big data challenges affect the business world in ways first experienced in the sciences decades ago.

You can find the term big data in many business settings. It appears in advertisements for boot camps, draws attendees to conferences, and perplexes business leaders. Arguably, the term is ill-defined. A 1998 presentation given by John Mashey, then the Chief Scientist of Silicon Graphics, is often cited as the document that introduced the term (*Press, 2013*). The impact of big data on business is undeniable, despite its elusive meaning. There is a general agreement on the following three characteristics of big data, called the **3Vs**:

- **Volume**: The size of datasets has grown from megabytes to petabytes
- **Velocity**: The speed of data arrival has changed to near real time
- **Variety**: The sources of data have grown from structured databases to unstructured ones, such as social media, websites, audio, and video

Together these three characteristics pose a growing challenge to the business community. Data is stored in facilities across a vast network of local servers or relational databases. Virtual software access it with cloud-based applications. BI applications have typically included static dashboards based on fixed measures using structured data. Big data changes the business by affording a competitive advantage to those who can extract value from the large and rapidly changing sources of diverse data.

Today, people ask business analysts, *what is going to happen?* To answer this type of question, a business needs tools and processes to tap into the growing stream of data. Often this data will not fit into the existing databases without transformation. The continual need to acquire data requires a structured ETL approach to wrangle the unstructured nature of modern data. As you read this chapter, think about how companies may benefit from using the techniques presented, even when they are less complex than big data.

Use case: Bike Sharing, LLC

You will begin your exploration of BI and analytics through the lens of a fictional business called Bike Sharing, LLC. The company operates and maintains a fleet of publically rental bikes in the Washington D.C. metropolitan area. Their customers are typically from the urban area, including people from business, government, and universities. Customers enjoy the convenience of finding bikes easily within a network of bike-sharing stations throughout the city. Renters may rent a bicycle at one location and leave it at another station.

Bike Sharing, LLC started operations in 2011, and has enjoyed continued growth. They quickly established a BI group to keep track of the data collected about transactions, customers, and factors related to rentals, such as weather, holidays, and times of day. In 2014, they began to understand how they might use open source datasets to guide decisions regarding sales, operations, and advertising. In 2015, they expanded their BI talent pool with business analysts experienced with R and statistical methods that could use Bike Sharing data in new ways.

You joined Bike Sharing just a few months ago. You have a basic understanding of R from the many courses and tutorials that you used to expand your skills. You are working with a good group that has a diverse skillset, including programming, databases, and business knowledge. The first data you have been given is bike rental data covering the two-year period from Jan 1, 2011 to Dec 31, 2012 (*Kaggle, 2014*). You can download this same `Ch1_bike_sharing_data.csv` file from the book's website at h ttp://jgendron.github.io/com.packtpub.intro.r.bi/.

Data sources often include a data dictionary to help new users understand the contents and coding of the data.
Data Dictionary for Bike Sharing Data (*Kaggle, 2014*):

- `datetime`: Hourly date + timestamp
- `season`: 1 = spring, 2 = summer, 3 = fall, 4 = winter
- `holiday`: Whether the day is considered a holiday
- `workingday`: Whether the day is neither a weekend nor holiday
- `weather`:
    - 1: Clear, Few clouds, Partly cloudy, Partly cloudy
    - 2: Mist + Cloudy, Mist + Broken clouds, Mist + Few clouds, Mist
    - 3: Light Snow, Light Rain + Thunderstorm + Scattered clouds, Light Rain + Scattered clouds
    - 4: Heavy Rain + Ice Pellets + Thunderstorm + Mist, Snow + Fog
- `temp`: Temperature in Celsius
- `atemp`: *Feels like* temperature in Celsius
- `humidity`: Relative humidity
- `windspeed`: Wind speed

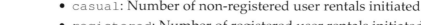

- casual: Number of non-registered user rentals initiated
- registered: Number of registered user rentals initiated
- count: Number of total rentals

One of your goals is to strengthen your ETL skills. In this use case, you will learn common extraction, transformation, and loading skills to store a dataset in a file for analysis. Welcome to the Bike Sharing team.

Extracting data from sources

Now we get to work. The aim of this book is to design, develop, and deliver a business intelligence product-a data product. In this section, you will explore two extraction methods to import data from different types of sources:

- Importing CSV and other file formats
- Importing data from relational databases

Depending on your background, you may be more or less familiar with both types of extraction methods. Here, you will learn or refresh your knowledge of both in order to have a more complete working understanding of ETL.

Importing CSV and other file formats

You can load the Bike Sharing data file into the R environment by using the read.csv() function. It is an easy and commonly used way to load CSV files:

```
bike <- read.csv("{filename}.csv")
```

Calling this function will read the file as long as it is located in your R working directory. The **working directory** is the space R uses, much like a home directory. There are two commands that you can use to check and change your working directory:

- getwd(): This will return the current working directory as a path in the R console
- setwd(<path>): This is used in the console to change the working directory to <path> you pass in the function

If you try to read a file that is not in your working directory, you will see an error message. Some analysts manage data in a separate data directory, one level under their working directory. In this case, you can add a path in front of the filename. The following example shows how the data file is located one layer down in a `data` directory. Adding the `./data/` string to the front of the filename will allow R to access the data:

```
bike <- read.csv("./data/Ch1_bike_sharing_data.csv")
str(bike)
```

The `str()` function is not required to import the data, but it does provide a confirmation that the data was read into the R environment. It also provides you with a quick look at the structure of the dataset, its dimensions, and the names of the variables:

```
'data.frame':   17379 obs. of  12 variables:
 $ datetime   : Factor w/ 17379 levels "1/1/2011 0:00",..: 1 2 13   ...
 $ season     : int  1 1 1 1 1 1 1 1 1 1 ...
 $ holiday    : int  0 0 0 0 0 0 0 0 0 0 ...
 $ workingday : int  0 0 0 0 0 0 0 0 0 0 ...
 $ weather    : int  1 1 1 1 1 2 1 1 1 1 ...
 $ temp       : num  9.84 9.02 9.02 9.84 9.84 ...
 $ atemp      : num  14.4 13.6 13.6 14.4 14.4 ...
 $ humidity   : int  81 80 80 75 75 75 80 86 75 76 ...
 $ windspeed  : num  0 0 0 0 0 ...
 $ casual     : int  3 8 5 3 0 0 2 1 1 8 ...
 $ registered : int  13 32 27 10 1 1 0 2 7 6 ...
 $ count      : int  16 40 32 13 1 1 2 3 8 14 ...
```

The `read.csv()` function uses default parameters that are consistent with CSV files, such as using a comma (,) as a separator. The R environment has a more flexible read option for instances when you may have tab-delimited data or TXT file. This option is the `read.table()` function:

```
bike <- read.table("./data/Ch1_bike_sharing_data.csv", sep = ",",
                    header = TRUE)
```

This function performs identically to the `read.csv()` function. In fact, `read.csv()` is built on `read.table()` and uses `sep = ","` and `header = TRUE` as default parameters.

Importing data from relational databases

You can also use R to access the data stored in many relational databases through the **Open Database Connectivity** (**ODBC**) application programming interface. In R, you do this using the `RODBC` package. This package provides you with an advantage for legacy data. By establishing an R connection to relational databases at Bike Sharing, LLC, you can reuse existing SQL-type queries that may already exist in the BI group.

Imagine that the Bike Sharing dataset was not a CSV file, but it was instead stored in a relational database. You can access the data by loading the `RODBC` package and establishing a connection to the database using the following parameters: data source name, user ID, and password. In this notional example, the user `Paul` would like to access the data source `ourDB` using his password `R4BI`:

```
library(RODBC)
connection <- odbcConnect(dsn = "ourDB", uid = "Paul", pwd = "R4BI")
```

As you follow along with this code, you will only be able to run the `odbcConnect()` function if you have configured a database source. Advanced users may try this using an Excel file. A tutorial for Windows-based environments is provided by Cyberfella LTD (2013) at `http://www.cyberfella.co.uk/212/6/11/windows7-odbc/`.

Having established a connection to your database, you can use R to write a SQL query, pass this query to the `sqlQuery()` function, and read the data into a `bike` data frame. You learned that there is a table in the database called `marketing`:

```
query <- "SELECT * FROM marketing"
bike <- sqlQuery(connection, query)
close(connection)
```

The `close()` function closes the connection between R and the database. Doing this will free any memory consumed by the open connection. It is a good practice to follow.

R tip: One thing you can do when establishing connections is to add a log to record your ETL processes. In the event something goes wrong, the log will capture the issue and help you find the problem quickly. The `log4r` package is specifically written for this application. For more information, visit the repository at `https://github.com/johnmyleswhite/log4r`.

There are also non-relational databases in the work place. **Non-relational databases** store documents, key value data, and unstructured data. Unlike the relational database approach, they contain different data structures grouped into nodes, clusters, or other schemas. The R community has created various packages to connect with non-relational databases and distributive filing systems. You can connect to MongoDB using the `rmongodb` package and to Spark distributed computing using the `SparkR` package.

BI tip: By looking at the database approach used within an organization and conceptualizing the data, a business analyst can better understand business processes to improve the quality of analysis and meet organizational needs.

Transforming data to fit analytic needs

In the previous section, you learned how to extract data and import it into R from various sources. Now you can transform it to create subsets of the data. This is useful to provide other team members with a portion of the data they can use in their work without requiring the complete dataset. In this section, you will learn the following four key activities associated with transformation:

- Filtering data rows
- Selecting data columns
- Adding a calculated column from existing data
- Aggregating data into groups

You will learn how to use functions from the `dplyr` package to perform data manipulation. If you are familiar with SQL, then `dplyr` is similar in how it filters, selects, sorts, and groups data. If you are not familiar with SQL, do not worry. This section will introduce you to the `dplyr` package. Learn more about the `dplyr` package by typing `browseVignettes(package = "dplyr")` into your R console.

Request from marketing: Marketing would like an extract from the data with revenues during the spring and summer seasons from days when only casual users rent bikes. They want a small CSV file with just the number of casual renters and revenue grouped by season.

Filtering data rows

You will filter rows with dplyr using the `filter()` function to extract a subset of rows that meet the criteria defined with logical operators such as those shown in the following table (*RStudio, 2015*). Read more about this by typing `?Comparison` or `?base::Logic` in the R console:

Logical Operators in the R Environment			
<	Less than	>	Greater than
<=	Less than or equal to	>=	Greater than or equal to
==	Equal to	!=	Not equal to
%in%	Group membership	&, |, !, xor, any, and all	Boolean operators
is.na	Is NA	!is.na	Is not NA

You can use these operators to pass a criterion, or many criteria, into your filter. Marketing would like to know how many times during spring or summer that only casual users rented bikes. You can begin creating a subset of the data by using the `filter()` function along with the == operator and the *or* Boolean (\|). Place the results in a temporary `extracted_rows` data frame:

```
library(dplyr)
extracted_rows <- filter(bike, registered == 0,
                         season == 1 | season == 2)
dim(extracted_rows)
```

We get the following output:

```
[1] 10 12
```

The `dim()` function call shows only `10` observations meet the filter criteria. This demonstrates the power of filtering larger datasets.

There are various ways of transforming the data. You can create an identical dataset using the `%in%` operator. This operator looks at each row (observation) and determines whether it is a member of the group based on criteria you specify. The first parameter is the name of the data frame, the second and successive parameters are filtering expressions:

```
using_membership <- filter(bike, registered == 0, season %in% c(1, 2))
identical(extracted_rows, using_membership)
```

We get the output as follows:

```
[1] TRUE
```

The `identical()` function compares any two R objects and returns `TRUE` if they are identical and `FALSE` otherwise. You created a subset of data by filtering rows and saving it in a separate data frame. Now you can select columns from that.

Selecting data columns

The `select()` function extracts columns you desire to retain in your final dataset. The marketing team indicated they were only interested in the season and casual renters. They did not express interest in environmental conditions or holidays. Providing team members data products that meet their specification is an important way to sustain relationships.

You can extract the required columns from `extracted_rows` and save these in another temporary `extracted_columns` data frame. Pass the `select()` function, data frame, and names of the columns to extract, `season` and `casual`:

```
extracted_columns <- select(extracted_rows, season, casual)
```

The following table provides a view of the first two observations from the subset data frame you generated. You notice that there is something missing. Marketing wants to know the number of casual renters and revenue by season. There is no revenue variable in the data you are using. What can you do about this? You can add a column to the data frame, as described in the following section:

	season	casual
1	1	2
2	1	1

Adding a calculated column from existing data

For your particular situation, you will be adding a calculated column. You asked marketing about the structure of rental costs and learn that casual renters pay five dollars for a day pass. You figured out that all you have to do is multiply the number of casual renters by five to get the revenues for each day in your data frame.

The mutate() function will calculate and add one or more columns, depending on the parameters. Your parameters include the data frame and an expression indicating the name of the new column and the calculation to create the revenue:

```
add_revenue <- mutate(extracted_columns, revenue = casual * 5)
```

The output will be as follows:

	season	casual	revenue
1	1	2	10
2	1	1	5
3	1	4	20
4	1	1	5
5	1	1	5
6	1	1	5
7	1	1	5
8	1	3	15
9	2	3	15
10	2	1	5

Perfect! You are nearly done. All you have left to do is to group and summarize the data into a final data frame.

Aggregating data into groups

The dplyr package provides you the group_by() and summarise() functions to help you aggregate data. You will often see these two functions used together. The group_by() function takes the data frame and variable on which you would like to group the data as parameters, in your case, season:

```
grouped <- group_by(add_revenue, season)
```

The `summarise()` function takes the data frame and all the variables you want to summarize as parameters. This also requires you to specify how you would like to summarize them. You may chose an average, minimum, maximum, or sum. Marketing wants to know total rentals and revenue by season, so you will use the `sum()` function:

```
report <- summarise(grouped, sum(casual), sum(revenue))
```

We get the output as follows:

	season	sum(casual)	sum(revenue)
1	1	14	70
2	2	4	20

This looks like it is what the marketing group wants. Now you have to deliver it.

R tip: There are many other transformation functions provided by the `dplyr` package. You can type `??dplyr` in your R console to get more information.

Loading data into business systems for analysis

You have imported and transformed data. It resides within your R environment as a data frame. Now you will need to provide it to marketing. The following are two common ways to export data from R into a file for use elsewhere in an organization:

- Writing data to a CSV file
- Writing data to a tab-delimited text file

These methods are similar, but they produce different results. Knowing about them and their differences will help you decide the format you would like to use.

Writing data to a CSV file

CSV files are common among data applications. Other data applications, such as Excel, can read these types of file. CSV files are also useful because database systems can typically import them into their environment, just as you imported a CSV into the R environment. The `write.csv()` function is used to write a data frame to a CSV file. In this example, the input parameters include `report` and the name of the output file, `revenue_report.csv`:

```
write.csv(report, "revenue_report.csv", row.names = FALSE)
```

You also used a `row.names = FALSE` parameter. Very often, your dataset will not contain row names. This parameter prevents R from adding a column of numerical identifiers to the CSV file. There are many other parameters you can use with `write.csv()`. Learn more about them by typing `?write.csv` in the R console.

Writing data to a tab-delimited text file

There may be times when you would like to have your data read by a data application that does not import CSV files. Recall that in the *Extracting data from sources* section, that `read.csv()` had a more flexible counterpart, `read.table()`. The `write.table()` function provides you with greater flexibility on how the final file is composed:

```
write.table(report, "revenue_report.txt", row.names = FALSE, sep = "\t")
```

The `write.table()` function uses a syntax that is very similar to `write.csv()`. You see the addition of `sep = "\t"`. This tells R to separate data with the tab character when creating the text file. There are many other parameters you can use with `write.table()`. Learn more about them by typing `?write.table` in the R console.

Summary

You completed the first step in your journey and should be pleased with yourself as ETL is not trivial or simple. In this chapter, you learned how to execute an ETL process from start to finish. This includes knowing how to extract data from multiple sources, including databases. Then, you transformed the data with the `dplyr` package and exported the information into a file that could be loaded into a business system.

In the next chapter, you will learn how to clean data once it is loaded. You will see that, like ETL, data cleaning is a broad and multi-faceted aspect of business intelligence and analytics.

2

Data Cleaning

Clean data is an essential element of good data analysis. Poor data quality is a primary reason for problems in business intelligence analysis. **Data cleaning** is the process of transforming raw data into usable data. Cleaning data, checking quality, and standardizing data types accounts for the majority of an analytic project schedule.

Anthony Goldbloom, the CEO of Kaggle, said: *Eighty percent of data science is cleaning data and the other twenty percent is complaining about cleaning data (personal communication, February 14, 2016).*

This chapter covers four key topics using some of the newer packages available within the R environment:

- Summarizing your data for inspection
- Finding and fixing flawed data
- Converting inputs to data types suitable for analysis
- Adapting string variables to a standard

Business analysts spend a lot of time cleaning data before moving to the analysis phase. Data cleaning does not have to be a dreaded task. This chapter provides business analysts with a structured process called **summarize-fix-convert-adapt** to turn raw data into datasets ready for analysis.

Summarizing your data for inspection

We live in an information age. Large and accessible datasets are being widely used in business intelligence and decision making. When you begin the data cleaning process, you will need a way of summarizing your data. You will need to understand its content and structure at the beginning of the process. Large datasets require ways of summarizing the data for inspection. Fortunately, the R language provides them for you! You will learn data cleaning through a use case called the **Bike Sharing Analysis Project**.

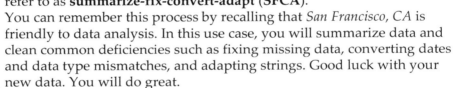

Use case: Bike Sharing Analysis Project

Imagine you are a business analyst on the Bike Sharing Analysis Project. New data has just arrived for analysis. Unlike the dataset you saw in `Chapter 1`, *Extract, Transform, and Load*, which was pre-processed for a Kaggle competition, this data you received has arrived in raw form. The book's website at `http://jgendron.github.io/com.packtpub.intro.r.bi/` contains the `Ch2_raw_bikeshare_data.csv` data. Before you start the analysis phase, you must do your due diligence to clean the data to get it ready. We will follow a four-step, structured approach that the authors refer to as **summarize-fix-convert-adapt** (SFCA).

You can remember this process by recalling that *San Francisco, CA* is friendly to data analysis. In this use case, you will summarize data and clean common deficiencies such as fixing missing data, converting dates and data type mismatches, and adapting strings. Good luck with your new data. You will do great.

The first step in data cleaning is to look at the data in a larger context. You do this by learning as much as you can about the data from what fits on your screen. In other words, you summarize the data.

Summarizing using the str() function

The R language is a powerful statistical computing environment. It is also a very good data inspection tool. In `Chapter 1`, *Extract, Transform, and Load*, you learned how to read a comma-separated value data file as a data frame. Now, you will assign your dataset to a data frame called `bike` and use the `str()` function to summarize and inspect the data frame:

```
bike <- read.csv("./data/Ch2_raw_bikeshare_data.csv",
                stringsAsFactors = FALSE)
str(bike)
```

This function will increase your understanding of the data with a small amount of code.

 BI tip: Data is a powerful way to provide business intelligence. Key stakeholders gain insights from data to make educated decisions. Data must fit the organization's situation and format to be most useful. Data cleaning is the largest and hardest part of any business intelligence or data analytic project. The success of data to inform organizations rests in the skills of the business analyst.

Inspecting and interpreting your results

A small screen of content will appear in the R console. This screen summary of the data appears here for inspection:

```
'data.frame':   17379 obs. of  13 variables:
 $ datetime  : chr  "1/1/2011 0:00" "1/1/2011 1:00" "1/1/2011  ...
 $ season    : int  1 1 1 1 1 1 1 1 1 1 ...
 $ holiday   : int  0 0 0 0 0 0 0 0 0 0 ...
 $ workingday: int  0 0 0 0 0 0 0 0 0 0 ...
 $ weather   : int  1 1 1 1 1 2 1 1 1 1 ...
 $ temp      : num  9.84 9.02 9.02 9.84 9.84 ...
 $ atemp     : num  14.4 13.6 13.6 14.4 14.4 ...
 $ humidity  : chr  "81" "80" "80" "75" ...
 $ windspeed : num  0 0 0 0 0 ...
 $ casual    : int  3 8 5 3 0 0 2 1 1 8 ...
 $ registered: int  13 32 27 10 1 1 0 2 7 6 ...
 $ count     : int  16 40 32 13 1 1 2 3 8 14 ...
 $ sources   : chr  "ad campaign" "www.yahoo.com" "www.google.fi" ...
```

You can immediately interpret some key characteristics of the bike sharing data:

- 17379 observations and 13 variables
- Three data types: three character (chr), seven integer (int), and three numeric (num)
- The first observations of each variable give you a sense of the content

We now have an idea of what the dataset contains. We can also see some problems with the data. The dates are characters. In addition, the `humidity` variable is numeric, but it is stored as a character data type. There must be something causing the problems with these columns. Other functions allow views of the same characteristics in different ways:

- `dim()` provides you with the row and column dimensions of a data frame
- `head()` shows the top six lines of the data frame to see the surrounding data
- `tail()` shows the bottom six lines of the data frame

Take the opportunity to try these and other functions found in `Appendix B`, *Other Helpful R Functions*. Begin creating your own style when summarizing data. This section gave you an insight to start fixing the data.

Finding and fixing flawed data

The summarize step revealed some possible flaws in the data. Mind you, the bike sharing data is in good shape compared to many datasets that you will encounter as a business analyst. Your next step in the SFCA approach is to fix any flaws that could impact your analysis. First, you have to find the flaws before you can fix them.

Finding flaws in datasets

There is no single best way to find flaws in data. This activity requires art mixed with some computational methods. The approach presented in this section shares some methods, but they only represent a few of the many possible ways of finding flawed data.

R tip: Keep an open mind and strive to become a lifelong learner of business analytics. The methods change and adapt continually. The best business analysts have a skillset that goes beyond great coding. Throughout this book, the authors will share their favorite picks from videos, blogs, and books relevant to the chapters.

One tip for business analysts is to find R packages that help you accomplish your job. There are many R packages out there. As the saying goes, for most data problems, there is an R package. How many R packages exist? On June 18, 2015, Joseph Rickert counted 6,789 of them (*Vries, 2015*). These packages continue to evolve and build upon one another. For instance, the first package you will use to clean the data is `stringr`, published in April 2015. Now, we will share it with you. You can learn more about it in the *Introduction to stringr* (*Wickham, 2015*) article. Load the package and start to look for the missing data. This is a very good place to start.

Missing values

Missing data-referred to as NA or null values-pose many difficulties for analysis methods. How do you find the average of NA? Finding missing data is so important that there are R functions specifically designed to find them. The `is.na()` function is optimized to search large datasets and quickly find missing values:

```
table(is.na(bike))
```

The output is as follows:

```
 FALSE    TRUE
225373     554
```

It looks like there are 554 NA values from the nearly quarter of a million elements in your data. That is not many, but you must deal with them. Your options include eliminating the problem observations or imputing the data. **Imputing data** means to repair the missing data based on some method: taking random samples, using a variable mean or group means, or generating values based on predictive models such as linear regression.

 Learn more: The imputation approach you choose depends on the randomness of the missing data and your knowledge. Imputing data can be simple or difficult-multiple chapters of various books are devoted to data imputation. Where is the missing data? What variable(s) include NA values? You can learn more about imputation in *Chapter 25* of *Data Analysis Using Regression and Multilevel/Hierarchical Models* (*Gelman & Hill, 2006*).

The `stringr` package has a set of functions to detect strings. You can use the package in this case as the `NA` value is a string within the dataset. Running the `str_detect()` function will look for all values of the `NA` string in the `bike` data frame:

```
library(stringr)
str_detect(bike, "NA")
```

We will get the output as follows:

```
 [1] FALSE FALSE FALSE FALSE FALSE FALSE FALSE FALSE FALSE FALSE
[11] FALSE FALSE TRUE
```

You interpret the output of the `str_detect()` function in the following way:

- The `NA` string was not detected in variables 1 through 12
- The `TRUE` value in the 13th position indicates column 13 contains `NA` values

Entering the R code `table(is.na(bike$sources))` produces a table similar to the one you created with `table(is.na(bike))` with 554 matches. This means that all 554 `NA` values are in the `sources` variable. You will need some additional string manipulation skills to fix this error. We will teach you that skill in the *Adapting string variables to a standard* section a few pages from now.

Erroneous values

You found that the `humidity` variable was problematic when you reviewed the data summary. `humidity` is a numerical value, but the summary showed it stored as a character data type. You will now determine what is causing the problem in this column.

One strategy that you can use is to search for all instances of character values in `humidity` and save them to a `bad_data` object. The `str_subset()` function of `stringr` applies a **regular expression** string to a column and extracts all matching instances into an object:

```
bad_data <- str_subset(bike$humidity, "[a-z A-Z]")
```

Regular expressions are a lexicon made up of characters and symbols to form powerful search strings. You can learn more about this useful topic in the Hadley Wickham (*2015*) article, *Introduction to stringr*.

Printing the `bad_data` object reveals a single error where the `x61` value is included in the column. You are familiar with the idea of imputing data and are aware that the technique can be misused. In this case, it appears that the error is typographical and you choose to impute the value rather than eliminate the row. Passing the elements of `bad_data` into the `str_detect()` function will assign the row position of `x61` to `location`:

```
location <- str_detect(bike$humidity, bad_data)
```

 Learn more: Other erroneous values can occur from **encoding**-the way text characters are stored in memory. URLs such as this example, `.../cat%20pictures.html` encode *space* as `%20`. Encoding styles include ASCII, ANSI, and UTF-8. Encoding can turn a seemingly simple analysis into a challenge. Encoding may introduce hard-to-find erroneous values, such as unknown encoding or misrepresented encoding, into the data (*Levy, 2013*).

Using subsetting `[ , ]` in R allows you to inspect just those observations that contain the erroneous value. You can expect to see a single instance, but you want to know where:

```
bike[location, ]
```

The output is as follows:

```
            datetime season holiday workingday weather   temp atemp
14177 8/18/2012 21:00      3       0          0       1 27.06 31.06
         humidity windspeed casual registered count      sources
14177         x61         0     90        248   338 www.bing.com
```

See how R allows you to navigate data with purpose. No need to search aimlessly with functions. No need to scour endless spreadsheets. The four-step structured SFCA approach helped you find a flaw in the row `14177`. Now you can fix it.

Fixing flaws in datasets

The `stringr` package also contains a `str_replace_all()` function to replace strings based on criteria you provide as input parameters to the function:

```
bike$humidity <- str_replace_all(bike$humidity, bad_data, "61")
```

Again, you will use subsetting to inspect the results. Did you successfully fix the `humidity` variable by replacing the single instance of `bad_data` with the new `61` string?

```
bike[location, ]
```

Typing that code will return the following output:

```
            datetime season holiday workingday weather  temp atemp
14177 8/18/2012 21:00      3       0          0       1 27.06 31.06
      humidity windspeed casual registered count    sources
14177       61         0     90        248   338 www.bing.com
```

Yes! You did a good job. You have learned a basic strategy to fix data. Now, you will need strategies for those times when data does not contain a flaw, but its form is not useful for your analysis design. This is when you want to convert the data.

Converting inputs to data types suitable for analysis

Another aspect of data cleaning is investigating the input data and shaping it to conform to your analysis design needs. The third step of the SFCA approach is convert. Specifically, converting the data from one data type to another.

Converting between data types

The R environment stores data in one of the several data types. You will experience five different data types in the Bike Sharing Analysis Project:

Data type	Explanation	Example
Numeric	A number having a decimal value	`9.84`
Integer	A number without decimals	`3`
Character	A string variable	`"www.google.com"`
Factor	A categorical variable that has a character and integer representation	`"ad campaign", "blog": 1,2`
Date	A date or time in various formats	`2016-02-16 18:56:57 EST`

Each data type has different properties consistent with definitions used in disciplines such as computer science, mathematics, and statistics. Some R library packages require input data to arrive as a certain type. When you have data that does not conform to an R library requirement, or your analysis design, you can convert it to another type. The data for the Bike Sharing Analysis Project requires the following three conversions:

- **Character to Numeric**: The typographic error in the `humidity` data coerced it to a character type, but you need to convert it back to numeric.

- **Character to Factor**: A common strategy for using `read.csv()` is to set `stringsAsFactors = FALSE`. This means categorical features are not automatically detected and you will later choose which ones are factors.

- **Character to Date**: A common situation is incorrect date conversion during file read. All your dates are characters. This is a difficult conversion, but it is detailed in the *Date and time conversions* section.

The first two conversions are relatively easy, so you begin there. R contains a family of type conversion functions. They take the general `as.{type}()` form, where `type` is the conversion applied. You will apply the `as.numeric()` function to the `humidity` variable:

```
bike$humidity <- as.numeric(bike$humidity)
```

Next, you will apply the `factor()` function to four variables that are actually categorical variables. First, you will apply a simple factor conversion to the two nominal scale variables, `holiday` and `workingday`. Using the `levels = c(0, 1)`, `labels = c("no", "yes")` parameters will also transform the numerical labels into human-readable values:

```
bike$holiday <- factor(bike$holiday, levels = c(0, 1),
                       labels = c("no", "yes"))
bike$workingday <- factor(bike$workingday, levels = c(0, 1),
                          labels = c("no", "yes"))
```

For the ordinal scale variables, `season` and `weather`, you will set the factor using an R capability called ordered factors. Like the previous transformation, provide `levels` and `labels` parameters. You can also place `levels` in the order you desire. For instance, you may like the seasons ordered as `spring`, `summer`, `fall`, and `winter`. If you do not force an order, R orders factors alphabetically. You will force the ordering with `ordered = TRUE`:

```
bike$season <- factor(bike$season, levels = c(1, 2, 3, 4),
                      labels = c("spring", "summer",
                                 "fall", "winter"),
                      ordered = TRUE)
```

```
bike$weather <- factor(bike$weather, levels = c(1, 2, 3, 4),
                      labels = c("clr_part_cloud",
                                 "mist_cloudy",
                                 "lt_rain_snow",
                                 "hvy_rain_snow"),
                  ordered = TRUE)
```

Nice work! Now you can tackle a very common data type conversion-dates and times. Here we will demonstrate another recently updated R package called lubridate, published in December, 2015. You can learn more by reading *Dates and Times Made Easy with lubridate* (*Grolemund & Wickham, 2011*). We also recommend you that consult the package documentation for more information about date and time conversions. They can be very tricky and can cause a great deal of frustration when using them; however, they are powerful when used correctly.

Date and time conversions

The secret to successful date conversions is to know the date form in the input dataset. You can run various R functions to view the form of the datetime variable. However, when you were fixing the humidity variable in row 14177, you may recall the datetime variable was in the 8/18/2012 21:00 format. Expressed in general terms, it has the {m/dd/yyyy hh:mm} form. Functions in the lubridate package are named using letters representing the order of the input data. With your dataset, you will use the mdy_hm() function:

```
library(lubridate)
bike$datetime <- mdy_hm(bike$datetime)
```

Using the str() function will produce the following output:

```
'data.frame':   17379 obs. of  13 variables:
 $ datetime  : POSIXct, format: "2011-01-01 00:00:00" ...
 $ season    : Ord.factor w/ 4 levels "spring"<"summer"<..: 1 1 1 ...
 $ holiday   : Factor w/ 2 levels "no","yes": 1 1 1 1 1 1 1 1 1 1 ...
 $ workingday: Factor w/ 2 levels "no","yes": 1 1 1 1 1 1 1 1 1 1 ...
 $ weather   : Ord.factor w/ 4 levels "clr_part_cloud"<..: 1 1 1  ...
 $ temp      : num  9.84 9.02 9.02 9.84 9.84 ...
 $ atemp     : num  14.4 13.6 13.6 14.4 14.4 ...
 $ humidity  : num  81 80 80 75 75 75 80 86 75 76 ...
 $ windspeed : num  0 0 0 0 0 ...
 $ casual    : int  3 8 5 3 0 0 2 1 1 8 ...
 $ registered: int  13 32 27 10 1 1 0 2 7 6 ...
 $ count     : int  16 40 32 13 1 1 2 3 8 14 ...
 $ sources   : chr  "ad campaign" "www.yahoo.com" "www.google.fi" ...
```

Adapting string variables to a standard

You are almost done with the basics of data cleaning. At this point in the process, you have summarized, fixed, and converted your input data. This means that it is time for you to accomplish the fourth SFCA step, adapting your data to a standard.

The term standard has many possible meanings. It may be that an R package will set a standard for you. In other cases, you may wish to establish one. For instance, notice in the previous data view that the `sources` variable is a character data type. You will see that it contains the advertising source where the customer learned about bike sharing. Leaving this as a character data type seems reasonable, but R cannot group character items to summarize them in analysis.

Your implied standard is that `sources` should be a categorical variable. What might happen if you use the `as.factor(bike$sources)` function? This will convert the data, but before you do that, you should consider a couple of questions:

- How many unique kinds of advertising source are in `sources`?
- How many categories would you like to have in your analysis dataset?

You can answer the first question with `unique(bike$sources)` to see all unique values:

```
 [1] "ad campaign"     "www.yahoo.com"   "www.google.fi"
 [4] "AD campaign"     "Twitter"         "www.bing.com"
 [7] "www.google.co.uk" "facebook page"  "Ad Campaign"
[10] "Twitter    "     NA               "www.google.com"
[13] "direct"          "blog"
```

It is worth discussing this output in detail to understand data adaption before we perform any string manipulation. What do you see in the results?

Observed	Explained
Two Twitter strings	Extra white space at element 10 treats these as different values
Multiple ad campaigns	R is case-sensitive-making elements 1, 4, and 9 all unique cases
The NA value	As discovered in the *Finding flaws in datasets* section

The `stringr` R package contains many functions to manipulate strings. The following code shows two functions, as well the use of subsetting to convert all strings to lower case, trim excess white space, and replace all NA values with the `unknown` string:

```
bike$sources <- tolower(bike$sources)
bike$sources <- str_trim(bike$sources)
na_loc <- is.na(bike$sources)
bike$sources[na_loc] <- "unknown"
```

Rerunning the `unique(bike$sources)` function produces the fruits of your labor. You have reduced the original 14 unique types of advertising source to 11, as follows:

```
 [1] "ad campaign"      "www.yahoo.com"    "www.google.fi"
 [4] "twitter"          "www.bing.com"     "www.google.co.uk"
 [7] "facebook page"    "unknown"          "www.google.com"
[10] "direct"           "blog"
```

This answers the first question. Now you need to determine how many unique kinds of advertising source you would like for your analysis. George Miller (*1956*) established *Miller's Law*. It states that the human mind works best with things and categories when they appear in quantities of seven, plus or minus two.

The power of seven, plus or minus two

Having eleven different advertising sources is not *bad* in the sense that there is no right or wrong answer. *Miller's Law* helps analysts think about analysis design. Consider histograms: too many categories is just as problematic as too few categories. For this project, you will decide to have five to nine categories of advertising sources in the dataset.

After talking with people experienced in advertising, you will learn that, when it comes to websites, the important thing is not which search engine they used. It is only important to know that the person found Bike Sharing services on the Web. You may decide to adapt all search engine sources by labeling them all as web. There is an R package for that.

The `DataCombine` package is a user-friendly library of functions to combine data into newly defined categories. The following code accomplishes this adaption:

```
library(DataCombine)
web_sites <- "(www.[a-z]*.[a-z]*)"
current <- unique(str_subset(bike$sources, web_sites))
replace <- rep("web", length(current))
```

The preceding code is described as follows:

- Assign a regular expression string into the web_sites variable, which is now a search string to find all variants of strings starting with www.
- Use str_subset() to find these instances and assign them to current.
- Create an instance of the web replacement string for each item contained in the current variable and assign them to replace. The length(current) function tells the code how many instances of web are needed. It should be as many as there are elements in current.

Create a cross-reference table by storing the current and replace variables as vectors in a replacements data frame:

```
replacements <- data.frame(from = current, to = replace)
```

The output is as follows:

	from	to
1	www.yahoo.com	web
2	www.google.fi	web
3	www.bing.com	web
4	www.google.co.uk	web
5	www.google.com	web

You are now ready to use the FindReplace() function to adapt the strings in bike$sources from five different Web search engine names to the web string. Notice how the FindReplace() function uses the from and to elements of the replacements data frame that you just created as input parameters to the function in the following code:

```
bike <- FindReplace(data = bike, Var = "sources", replacements,
                    from = "from", to = "to", exact = FALSE)
unique(bike$sources)
```

The output is as follows:

```
[1] "ad campaign"    "web"        "twitter"     "facebook page"
[5] "unknown"        "direct"     "blog"
```

Running the `unique()` function shows that you have reduced the original 14 unique types of advertising source down to 7. George Miller would be proud of you. The last thing to do is fully adapt the string variable by converting it to a factor with the `as.factor()` function:

```
bike$sources <- as.factor(bike$sources)
```

Data ready for analysis

You have completed the four-step SFCA structured approach to summarize, fix, convert, and adapt your data. A quick call of the `str(bike)` function shows you the data ready for analysis:

```
'data.frame':  17379 obs. of  13 variables:
$ datetime   : POSIXct, format: "2011-01-01 00:00:00" "2011-01-01 ...
$ season     : Ord.factor w/ 4 levels "spring"<"summer"<..: 1 1 1 ...
$ holiday    : Factor w/ 2 levels "no","yes": 1 1 1 1 1 1 1 1 1 1 ...
$ workingday : Factor w/ 2 levels "no","yes": 1 1 1 1 1 1 1 1 1 1 ...
$ weather    : Ord.factor w/ 4 levels "clr_part_cloud"<..: 1 1 1  ...
$ temp       : num  9.84 9.02 9.02 9.84 9.84 ...
$ atemp      : num  14.4 13.6 13.6 14.4 14.4 ...
$ humidity   : num  81 80 80 75 75 75 80 86 75 76 ...
$ windspeed  : num  0 0 0 0 0 ...
$ casual     : int  3 8 5 3 0 0 2 1 1 8 ...
$ registered : int  13 32 27 10 1 1 0 2 7 6 ...
$ count      : int  16 40 32 13 1 1 2 3 8 14 ...
$ sources    : Factor w/ 7 levels "ad campaign",..: 1 7 7 1 5 7 1 ...
```

This looks great! Finish your data cleaning process by writing the results to a CSV file. You learned how to use `write.csv()` in Chapter 1, *Extract, Transform, and Load*:

```
write.csv(bike,"Ch2_clean_bike_sharing_data.csv",
        row.names = FALSE)
```

Summary

Congratulations! You have learned a lot of topics in this chapter. Data cleaning is a very important part of business intelligence analysis. In this chapter, you learned that cleaning data is a four-step process that can be remembered by SFCA (summarize-fix-convert-adapt).

Summarizing the data gives you a big-picture overview and provides a perspective on the data. This shapes your data cleaning strategies. **Fixing** flawed data can be tedious, but there are common practices to use. **Converting** data is important to get it in the right data type to support your analysis. Dates and times can be difficult, but tools help with this. **Adapting** your data to a standard is the key to setting a foundation for a successful data analysis. Standards may be given or you may design one.

Continuing to learn is also important as the packages and methods change frequently. Lastly, the topic of data cleaning is full of interesting ideas that you may find helpful. A recommended resource is *An Introduction to Data Cleaning with R (Jonge & Loo, 2013)*.

This chapter ends *Part 1* of the book and concludes your learning about getting and cleaning data. *Part 2* contains four chapters to help you learn analysis techniques you will likely encounter in a business setting. For instance, in the next chapter, you will learn exploratory data analysis. This is where all your work pays off, as you can find trends and relationships that help determine the best analysis approach to solve the business needs with clean data.

3

Exploratory Data Analysis

One way to learn new things is through discovery. Exploratory data analysis is a term attributed to the statistician John Tukey in a book of the same name (*Tukey, 1977*). **Exploratory data analysis** means examining a dataset to discover its underlying characteristics with an emphasis on visualization. It helps you during analysis design to determine if you should gather more data, suggest hypotheses to test, and identify models to develop. In this chapter, we will cover the following four topics related to exploratory data analysis:

- Understanding exploratory data analysis
- Analyzing a single data variable
- Analyzing two variables together
- Exploring multiple variables simultaneously

You will learn common techniques that statisticians and analysts use to characterize data. These include tabular and graphical methods to explore the dataset. There are many interesting things to discover in a dataset, but in business or science you are exploring to determine the aspects of your data that will help build analytic models.

Use case: Questions About Bike Sharing, LLC

You have been working with Bike Sharing data for enough time to feel comfortable with its content and quality. Now the company's marketing manager has set up a meeting to talk to you. She wants to know more information from the data that will help drive some business decisions that her group is considering.

Although models are an important aspect of analytics, the process actually begins with a good question. You found that asking the right question is often the hardest part in solving a problem. You cannot simply ask the marketing manager, *what questions do you have for me?* It is not that easy. Therefore, you transform from a business analyst and take on the persona of a consultant and facilitator.

You will need to work with others who have expertise in the domain of marketing and you will interact with them to help them form good questions. The data that you will explore in this chapter is marketing data that you use for analysis in later chapters. The `Ch3_marketing.csv` file is available at the book's website:

`http://jgendron.github.io/com.packtpub.intro.r.bi/`

Bike Sharing LLC purchased an industry report containing business intelligence on 172 other bicycle rental operations gathered during an industry trends analysis. The dataset consists of 172 observations and 7 variables:

- Expenditures for Google AdWords advertising
- Expenditures for Facebook advertising
- Expenditures for Twitter advertising
- Total marketing budget
- Revenues associated with that specific facility
- Number of employees
- Market as defined by population density (Low, Medium, High)

This chapter provides you an opportunity to learn new skills, as well as a new way of looking at data problems. Good luck with your explorations.

Understanding exploratory data analysis

"An approximate answer to the right question is worth a great deal more than a precise answer to the wrong question."

– John Tukey

Exploratory data analysis is a fascinating area as it blends the art of conversation, skills of data science, and aspects of the domain being studied. It is a structured process where you discover information about the data characteristics and relationships among two or more variables.

Questions matter

The biostatistician, Roger Peng, has said that developing questions is a practical way of reducing the exponential number of ways you can explore a dataset. *In particular, a sharp question or hypothesis can serve as a dimension reduction tool that can eliminate variables that are not immediately relevant to the question (Peng, 2015, p. 17).*

The use case highlights the importance of asking good questions. Your success in conducting exploratory data analysis will rely on your skills as an investigator. For a moment, take on the persona of a journalist or researcher. They live in a world of questions and seek data to answer these questions. You can think of data science in the similar way. You may already have a sizable amount data, and it is tempting to dive right into it and start answering questions. How do you know the data is appropriate for answering the questions?

As you begin this chapter, consider this story. A philosopher had some students, and it was the end of their time together. He asked his students, *"so, what is the answer?"* His students looked around at each other, but no one spoke. The philosopher then asked the greater question, *"well, if no one has the answer, can someone at least tell me what the question is?"* The ultimate goal of analysis is communicating an answer to a question. The following figure shows a generalized data science pipeline from beginning to end:

Models and analysis are useful to the extent they answer a well-developed question. A key goal in business intelligence is providing **answers**, through **models**, to the **question**.

Scales of measurement

Sometimes, it is important to go back to the fundamentals of a discipline and remind ourselves of things that we think we understand so well. In this chapter, you will find it important to understand the scale of the data that you are working with. Data can be of different types, with each type having certain statistics associated with them, referred to as **scales of measurement**.

Stanley Stevens was a psychologist who coined the term *scales of measurement* (*Stevens, 1946*). He highlighted this topic in a paper that culminated a seven-year committee of the British Association for the Advancement of Science. Their task was to add meaning to measurement. The committee came up with four types of measurement scales: **nominal**, **ordinal**, **interval**, and **ratio**. It may be hard to believe, but people could not point to a standard on this matter until the middle of the last century.

The following table shows each scale, as well as what operations they allow and statistics permitted for each scale. Take a little time to review these scales as we will reference them in the chapter. In exploratory data analysis, it is important to understand scales of measurement when generating summary statistics and plots:

Scale	Basic empirical operations	Permissible statistics
Nominal	Determining equality or membership	Number of cases Mode Contingency correlation
Ordinal	Determining of greater than or less than	Median Percentiles
Interval	Determining equality of interval or difference	Mean Standard deviation Rank-order correlation Product-moment correlation
Ratio	Determining equality of ratios	Coefficient of variation

Here is an example to help explain the different scales. The following data is from a secondary school roster showing **gender**, **level**, **age**, and **grade point average** (**GPA**):

Gender	Level	Age	GPA
Male	Sophomore	15	3.6
Female	Freshman	14	3.2
Female	Sophomore	14	3.3
Male	Junior	16	3.7
Female	Senior	18	3.1
Male	Senior	17	2.8

The preceding data is described as follows:

- Gender is **nominal**. A student can be either a male or female. You can calculate the *count* and *mode* of nominal scale data.
- Level is **ordinal**. Seniors are above juniors, juniors are above sophomores, and sophomores are above freshmen. You can calculate the *median* and *percentiles* of ordinal scale data when represented numerically.
- Age is **interval**. Values are continuous with an understood increment between them. In this example, an integer represents a student's age and they differ by increments of one year. You can calculate the *mean* and *standard deviation* of interval scale data.
- GPA is a **ratio**. It is a combination of two other numbers expressed as a rational number.

The important thing to remember is that data belong to different scales. These scales allow certain types of operations and statistics, and are not suited for other types.

R data types

When data is loaded into R, it is assigned a data type. The following are the five most common data types you will encounter in your analyses:

- **Numeric**: A number with a decimal value (for example, 10.1 and 2.0). R uses numeric as the default data type for numbers, unless you define them as another data type. Numeric uses an interval scale. Most ratios are numeric.
- **Integer**: A number without a decimal value (for example, 10 and 2). Integers also use an interval scale. Numeric is the default data type in R, but you can coerce a numeric into an integer using the `as.integer()` function:

```
as.integer(10.0)
```

It will return the following output:

```
[1] 10
```

- **Character**: A representation of a string value in R. Single characters can be used, or multiple characters can be concatenated with the `cat()` function to form longer strings. These string objects use a nominal or ordinal scale. You can coerce a number to a character using the `as.character()` function:

```
as.character(10.1)
```

We will get the following output:

```
[1] "10.1"
```

- **Logical**: A value stored as either TRUE or FALSE. Logical values are often the result of an operation comparing two other values. Consider the following as an example:

```
10 == 2
```

The output is as follows:

```
[1] FALSE
```

- **Factor**: A factor applies to categorical variables, both nominal and ordinal. According to the R help information (available by typing ?factor() in the console), a factor encodes a vector of categories (character or numbers) in such a way that they are considered levels of this variable. These discrete labels are quite useful for grouping and filtering data based on categories.

R has two other data types, Complex and Raw, but these will not be discussed in this book. If you like to determine what data type your variable is stored in, you may apply the class() function to the variable and R will output its data type.

R tip: Data types are important to understand. R libraries and functions often require data to be of a certain type in order to execute. You will grow as an analyst as you spend time to become aware of the data types in your dataset and convert them when necessary, as described in Chapter 2, *Data Cleaning*.

Analyzing a single data variable

If your dataset has a single variable, you have univariate data. When examining univariate data, you may describe the data distribution in terms of its value and spread. A good place to begin the exploration of univariate data is with the str() function that you learned in Chapter 2, *Data Cleaning*. Load the marketing dataset into R and run the str() function:

```
marketing <- read.csv("./data/Ch3_marketing.csv", stringsAsFactors = TRUE)
str(marketing)
```

We will get the following output:

```
'data.frame':  172 obs. of  7 variables:
 $ google_adwords : num  65.7 39.1 174.8 34.4 78.2 ...
 $ facebook       : num  47.9 55.2 52 62 40.9 ...
 $ twitter        : num  52.5 77.4 68 86.9 30.4 ...
 $ marketing_total: num  166 172 295 183 150 ...
 $ revenues       : num  39.3 38.9 49.5 40.6 40.2 ...
 $ employees      : int  5 7 11 7 9 3 10 6 6 4 ...
 $ pop_density    : Factor w/ 3 levels "High","Low","Medium": 1 3 ...
```

You will see that it contains 172 observations of 7 variables. The first six variables are numeric, while the last is a factor having three levels: High, Low, and Medium. If you want the factor to have order, you must define the ordered factor. You created similar code in the last chapter. You can use this knowledge to convert pop_density into an ordered factor:

```
marketing$pop_density <- factor(marketing$pop_density,
                          ordered = TRUE,
                          levels = c("Low", "Medium", "High"))
```

Focus on two variables, google_adwords (interval, numeric) and pop_density (ordinal, factor). You can learn their distributions using a tabular or graphical approach.

Tabular exploration

This type of exploratory data analysis is relatively quick and consists of printing numbers on your console. The summary() function produces a five-number summary (plus the mean) for continuous variables. It also produces a count for categorical variables:

```
summary(marketing$google_adwords)
```

We will get the following output:

```
   Min. 1st Qu.  Median    Mean 3rd Qu.    Max.
  23.65   97.25  169.50  169.90  243.10  321.00
```

For any interval scale variable in the marketing dataset, the summary() function gives you what is known as the Tukey five-number summary (*Hoaglin* and others, *1983*) plus the mean. It provides you with the following information:

- **Minimum**: This is the smallest observation in the dataset
- **First Quartile**: 25% of the data lies below this value

- **Median**: This is the middle observation
- **Mean**: The average of the observations
- **Third Quartile**: 75% of the data lies below this value
- **Maximum**: This is the argest observation in the dataset

The five-number summary provides an easy-to-understand summary of how the data is distributed. It provides information about central tendency (the median), spread (the quartiles), and range (the minimum and maximum). By using the median instead of the mean, the five-number summary is applicable to ordinal measurements, as well as interval and ratio measurements. R also provides the variable's mean value. If you only want the five-number summary, you can use the `fivenum()` function.

As mentioned, R provides the mean along with the five-number summary. You can get the mean separately using the `mean()` function:

```
mean(marketing$google_adwords)
```

The output is as follows:

```
[1] 169.8685
```

You can also get two measures of spread that are often associated with the mean (standard deviation and variance) using the `sd()` and `var()` functions respectively:

```
sd(marketing$google_adwords)
```

We will get the standard deviation:

```
[1] 87.47228
```

If we use the following input:

```
var(marketing$google_adwords)
```

We will get the variance:

```
[1] 7651.4
```

You know quite a bit about your data now. For example, in the case of `google_adwords`, you know:

- The values range from a minimum of 23.65 to a maximum of 321
- 25% of the observations are below 97.25
- 50% of the observations are below 169.50 (the median)
- 75% of the observation are below 243.10

For the categorical `pop_density` variable, the `summary()` function only lists the three factor levels and the number of observations in each level. Notice that the factors are ordered based on the levels you set, not alphabetically as they were before you defined an order:

```
summary(marketing$pop_density)
```

The output is as follows:

```
   Low Medium   High
    68     52     52
```

Tabular exploration tells you quite a bit. Do you feel like you know as much as you could? Some things remain hidden until you plot them graphically.

Graphical exploration

> *"The greatest value of a picture is when it forces us to notice what we never expected to see."*
>
> *– John Tukey*

Getting summary statistics is important, but seeing the shape of your data is illuminating. Anscombe's Quartet is a classic example developed specifically to illustrate the value of data visualization (*Anscombe, 1973*). It is so classic, R comes with the data loaded:

```
data("anscombe")
anscombe
```

The following is the output:

```
   x1 x2 x3 x4    y1   y2    y3    y4
1  10 10 10  8  8.04 9.14  7.46  6.58
2   8  8  8  8  6.95 8.14  6.77  5.76
3  13 13 13  8  7.58 8.74 12.74  7.71
4   9  9  9  8  8.81 8.77  7.11  8.84
5  11 11 11  8  8.33 9.26  7.81  8.47
6  14 14 14  8  9.96 8.10  8.84  7.04
7   6  6  6  8  7.24 6.13  6.08  5.25
8   4  4  4 19  4.26 3.10  5.39 12.50
9  12 12 12  8 10.84 9.13  8.15  5.56
10  7  7  7  8  4.82 7.26  6.42  7.91
11  5  5  5  8  5.68 4.74  5.73  6.89
```

The interesting part about these four datasets is that the summary statistics (such as the mean, standard deviation, and variance) for each of the variables is near identical. The following is the console output of these descriptive statistics using the `sapply()` function, which applies another function, such as `mean()`, across all columns:

```
> sapply(anscombe, mean)
    x1     x2     x3     x4     y1     y2     y3     y4
9.0000 9.0000 9.0000 9.0000 7.5009 7.5009 7.5000 7.5009
> sapply(anscombe, sd)
    x1     x2     x3     x4     y1     y2     y3     y4
3.3166 3.3166 3.3166 3.3166 2.0316 2.0317 2.0304 2.0306
> sapply(anscombe, var)
     x1      x2      x3      x4      y1      y2      y3      y4
11.0000 11.0000 11.0000 11.0000  4.1273  4.1276  4.1226  4.1232
```

From this, you might conclude that these datasets are somehow similar, or even identical. Plotting the four datasets presents a very different picture, as shown here:

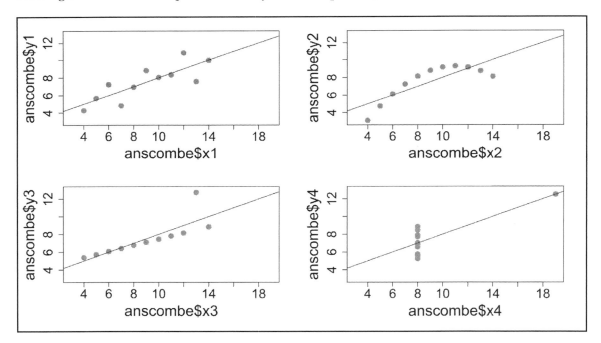

In the previous section, you explored your data by tabular inspection. Now, you will inspect your data using graphical techniques. You will use plots to inspect ordinal factors, such as `pop_density`. Boxplots and histograms present interval scale data, such as `google_adwords`.

Plot `pop_density` using the `plot()` function to visualize the values 68, 52, and 52:

```
plot(marketing$pop_density)
```

It will return the following output:

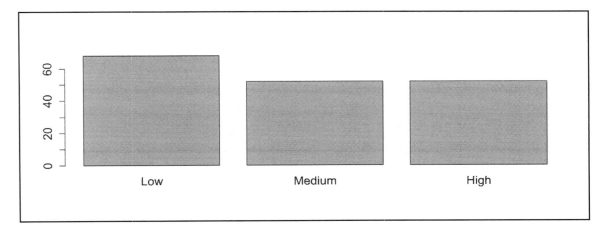

Now, explore the `google_adwords` variable using the `boxplot()` and `hist()` functions:

```
boxplot(marketing$google_adwords, ylab = "Expenditures")
hist(marketing$google_adwords, main = NULL)
```

The output is shown here:

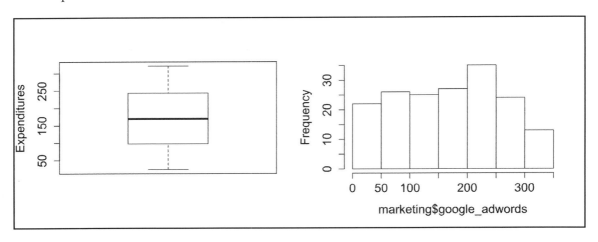

The left panel shows a boxplot with a thick horizontal line in the middle representing the median. You will see that it aligns with the value 169, which you found with tabular exploration. The upper and lower boundaries of the box correspond to the upper and lower quartiles, 243.10 and 97.25. The whiskers extend from the top and bottom of the box. In this case, they represent the maximum (321.00) and the minimum (23.65). This is not always the case, and the information in the following *boxplot whiskers* information box explains this. The boxplot is consistent with the five-number summary you extracted earlier.

The right panel is a histogram. It reveals what the tabular data and boxplot did not-the google_adwords variable is uniformly distributed. It is not a bell curve (normal curve). This information is still consistent with the boxplot and summary statistics, but a normal curve may have shown similar information. Notice the raw labelling on the x-axis of the histogram. This is all right in exploratory data analysis to create plots quickly.

Boxplot whiskers (optional and intermediate)
Boxplot whiskers are tricky. They do not necessarily represent the minimum and maximum values in the dataset, although they can. The top whisker represents whichever is *smaller*:

- *(a)*, the maximum value, *(321)*
- *(b)*, the value of the upper quartile, *(243.10) + (1.5 x IQR)*, where **IQR** is the **interquartile range**, or the difference between the upper quartile, *(243)*, and the lower quartile, *(97.25)*. This is *243 − 97.25 = 73.53*

In this case, the maximum value, *(a)*, is *321*. The alternate value is *(b) = 243 + (1.5 x 73.53) = 243 + 113.29 = 356.29*. The maximum value, *(a)*, of the range is smaller, therefore, this sets the upper whisker.

The top whisker represents whichever is *larger*:

- *(a)*, the minimum value, *(23.65)*
- *(b)*, the value of the lower quartile, *(97.25) – (1.5 x IQR)*

In this case, the minimum value, *(a)*, is *23.65*. The alternate value is *(b) = 97.25 – (1.5 x 73.53) = 97.25 – 109.87 = -12.62*. The minimum value, *(a)*, of the range is larger, therefore, this sets the lower whisker.

The `google_adwords` variable is uniform. How would a skewed variable appear in tabular and graphical form? It turns out the `twitter` variable is skewed. Go ahead and look at the tabular output using `summary(marketing$twitter)`:

```
   Min. 1st Qu.  Median    Mean 3rd Qu.    Max.
   5.89   20.94   34.60   38.98   52.94  122.20
```

Notice the difference between the median and the mean. This difference indicates skewed data. Plot the boxplot and histogram to see the skew using graphical exploration:

```
boxplot(marketing$twitter, ylab = "Expenditures", col = "gray")
hist(marketing$twitter, main = NULL, col = "blue")
```

We will get the following output:

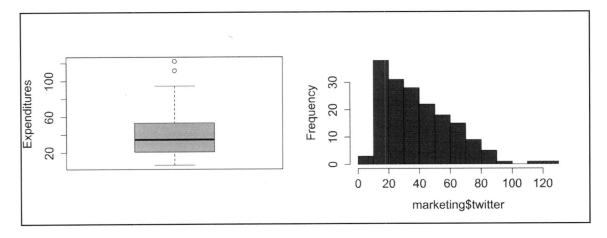

What do you notice different in these graphical inspections? Some data points in the boxplot appear as little bubbles above the upper whisker. This means that the upper whisker represents the IQR value and not the maximum value. This is a visual indication of the outliers. The two bubbles at the top of the boxplot appear in the histogram as the two values to the far right, straddling 120.

Learning graphics: You will see that color was added to the plots using the `col` parameter. Remember that you do not have to make your exploratory plots pretty. You will create many graphics in this phase. Focus on the information gain and you will professionalize the final graphics later. However, this chapter will show some graphics parameters so you will begin learning the key aspects of plotting in R.

The histogram in the right panel shows the right-skewed (positive) nature of the `twitter` variable. The skew is also visible in the boxplot. Notice that there are no bubbles on the lower whisker. When you see this combination, it may be an indication of skewness. You know this is the case based on your tabular data.

The following panels (adapted from *Johnson, n.d.*) show you the relationship of the mean and the median in normal versus skewed data. From left to right, the panels indicate left-skewed (negative) data, normally distributed data, and right-skewed (positive) data. Notice how the skew pulls the mean to the left or right and has less effect on the median:

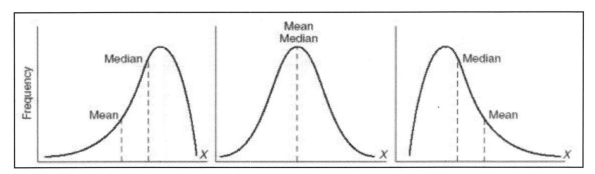

With a single variable, that is about all that you can do with the data analytically. If you have two variables, things become much more interesting.

Analyzing two variables together

If your dataset has two variables, you have bivariate data. When examining bivariate data, you want to explore possible relationships. This is where good questioning pays off. You can use the following four questions to guide your exploratory data analysis:

- What does the data *look* like?
- Is there any *relationship* between two variables?
- Is there any *correlation* between the two?
- Is the correlation *significant*?

Four words summarize these questions: *Look-Relationships-Correlation-Significance*. You will explore pairs of variables from the marketing dataset to investigate these questions using both tabular and graphical exploration methods.

What does the data look like?

This is something you know very well at this point. Summarize the data in your console as shown in the following:

```
summary(marketing)
```

The following is the output:

```
  google_adwords        facebook          twitter        marketing_total
 Min.   : 23.65     Min.   : 8.00     Min.   :  5.89     Min.   : 53.65
 1st Qu.: 97.25     1st Qu.:19.37     1st Qu.: 20.94     1st Qu.:158.41
 Median :169.47     Median :33.66     Median : 34.59     Median :245.56
 Mean   :169.87     Mean   :33.87     Mean   : 38.98     Mean   :242.72
 3rd Qu.:243.10     3rd Qu.:47.80     3rd Qu.: 52.94     3rd Qu.:322.62
 Max.   :321.00     Max.   :62.17     Max.   :122.19     Max.   :481.00
    revenues          employees       pop_density        emp_factor
 Min.   :30.45     Min.   : 3.000     Low   :68      (2.99,7.5]:78
 1st Qu.:40.33     1st Qu.: 6.000     Medium:52      (7.5,12]  :94
 Median :43.99     Median : 8.000     High  :52
 Mean   :44.61     Mean   : 7.866
 3rd Qu.:48.61     3rd Qu.:10.000
 Max.   :58.38     Max.   :12.000
```

Adding and removing variables: You may have noticed an extra column in this data. We added the `emp_factor` variable to show you plots between two variables that are factors. Here is how you can add variables to a data frame:

```
marketing$emp_factor <- cut(marketing$employees, 2)
```

There are two elements in this line of code. Look at what is going on here:

- The `cut()` function: This converts a number to a factor by dividing the values into a number of intervals you choose. In this case, you will pass in `marketing$employees` and tell R to cut it into two (2) factors. It splits the data at the midpoint between the minimum value (3) and the maximum value (12) resulting in a factor for 3 to 7 and 8 to 12 employees.
- Create a new variable: You can add new columns (variables) to a data frame by assigning the result of some operation to a new variable name. In this case, you used the `cut()` function and assigned the result to a new `emp_factor` variable using this new name as a variable.

The new variable is only there temporarily to show you some functionality in this section. You will remove it at the end of this section using the following code:

```
marketing$emp_factor <- NULL
```

Is there any relationship between two variables?

For context, imagine that you had two variables: the age and height of a group of people. You would expect a relationship between age and height. This can be shown with tabular exploration using the `table()` function. Create a table of the two factors, `emp_factor` and `pop_density`:

```
table(marketing$emp_factor, marketing$pop_density)
```

It will return the following output:

	Low	Medium	High
(2.99,7.5]	35	21	22
(7.5,12]	33	31	30

This gives you an idea of the relationship between these two factors. They appear balanced in both dimensions and you get a sense of the relationship of the factor variables with one another. The `table()` function works very well for factors, but not so well for numerical data. They can become quite large. Graphical exploration is helpful in these cases. There are three combinations of graphics when exploring bivariate variables:

```
mosaicplot(table(marketing$pop_density, marketing$emp_factor),
          col = c("gray","black"), main = "Factor / Factor")
boxplot(marketing$marketing_total ~ marketing$pop_density,
        main = "Factor / Numeric")
plot(marketing$google_adwords, marketing$revenues,
     main = "Numeric / Numeric")
```

The three combinations of graphics are shown here:

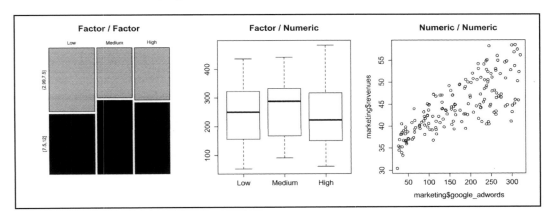

The three combinations are described as follows:

- **Factor/Factor**: You will plot two categorical factors using the `mosaicplot()` function. The data must first be placed in a `table()` object. In this case, you plotted the data same as the previous 3 x 2 table. Do you see the connection?
- **Factor/Numeric**: You will use the `boxplot()` function that you used earlier in this chapter to plot a categorical factor with a numeric variable. You will see in this middle panel that the total amount spent on marketing varies slightly from low to high population density locations. This plot demonstrates why you converted this factor into an ordered factor. If you had not ordered the factor, they would have alphabetically read along the bottom (**High, Low**, and **Medium**). Your work ordering the factor makes this more readable.

- **Numeric/Numeric**: Two numeric variables are plotted in a scatterplot using the `plot()` function. You pass the *x* dimension to the function first followed by the *y* dimension, separated by a comma. Scatterplots are helpful when visualizing relationships.

These tabular and graphical methods give you a glimpse into relationships between two variables. You may wish to explore other variables now, especially those that make sense to business questions. Now you focus on some relationships and ask the next question.

Is there any correlation between the two?

In two dimensions, you can answer this question quickly using the `cor()` function:

```
cor(marketing$google_adwords, marketing$revenues)
```

We will get the following output:

```
[1] 0.7662461
```

If we use the following input:

```
cor(marketing$google_adwords, marketing$facebook)
```

We will get the following output:

```
[1] 0.07643216
```

As you might have already guessed, this function provides you the correlation between two variables. The numerical result has two components, sign and value:

- **Sign** will either be positive (+) or negative (-). Positive correlation means that as the first variable increases, the second variable increases as well. Negative correlation means that when the first variable increases, the second variable decreases. Both the previous examples are positively correlated.
- **Value** of the correlation result ranges from zero (0) to one (1). The value increases as the correlation strength increases. The first example has a correlation of `0.766`, which is much stronger than the second example (`0.076`). A value of zero indicates no correlation between two variables.

With two variables, a simple tabular exploration may be sufficient. You will see the plots of these two examples later in this section. Keep these concepts in mind as you test the significance of correlations you find.

Is the correlation significant?

You may find strong or weak correlations. Now, you can determine whether a correlation is significant. In a statistical sense, significant means that your correlation is due to circumstances other than random chance.

In the last question, you saw that the correlation between `google_adwords` and `revenues` was `0.766`. This seems strong, especially when relative to the other correlation of `0.076`. You cannot determine significance by looking at a number alone. There is a statistical test included in R that will tell you whether a correlation is significant.

Run the test using the `cor.test()` function on `google_adwords` and `revenues` variables:

```
cor.test(marketing$google_adwords, marketing$revenues)
```

The output is as follows:

```
        Pearson's product-moment correlation
data:  marketing$google_adwords and marketing$revenues
t = 15.548, df = 170, p-value < 2.2e-16
alternative hypothesis: true correlation is not equal to 0
95 percent confidence interval:
 0.6964662 0.8216704
sample estimates:
      cor
0.7662461
```

There is a lot going on in this console output. When you use `cor.test()` on two variables, it conducts a t-test to examine something called the null hypothesis.

Learn more: If you have not learned about the null hypothesis and hypothesis testing, you should consider learning about it in order to understand this technique. The null hypothesis is at the heart of many analytic techniques that you have available in R. You can learn more about hypothesis testing online at Stat Trek or Khan Academy:

- http://stattrek.com/hypothesis-test/hypothesis-testing. aspx
- https://www.khanacademy.org/math/probability/statisti cs-inferential/hypothesis-testing/v/hypothesis-testin g-and-p-values

A **null hypothesis** typically represents the status quo-meaning that there is nothing going on. In our example, the null hypothesis is that the true correlation between `google_adwords` and `revenues` is equal to zero. In other words, the variables have no correlation. The **alternative hypothesis** is that the correlation between the two is not equal to zero and that the correlation is significant.

A **t-test** gets at the question: *how surprising is it to see this degree of correlation if the two variables truly are not correlated?* Going into the details of t-test is beyond the scope of this book, but the result of the t-test is `15.548`. How surprising is this result? The **p-value** associated with this value of `t` is `2.2e-16`. This essentially says, *if the null hypothesis were indeed true, the probability of getting t = 15.548 would be 0.00000000000000022.*

In other words, the probability of getting this result, if the null hypothesis were true, would essentially be zero. Therefore, you will reject the null hypothesis, stating that the correlation is zero. A typical value used for rejecting a null hypothesis is a p-value less than 0.05.

BI tip: Keep all this statistics stuff in perspective. Your goal is not to become a statistician. Rather, your goal is to become more aware of what your analysis means and what are its limitations. Business decisions are not the same as clinical drug trials, but you want to know when you can have faith in the analysis you provide to business leaders that informs their decisions.

Putting your business hat back on, you decide to determine whether the other two marketing channels (Twitter and Facebook) are correlated and significant. You run `cor.test()` on these variables against `revenues`. The following is a summary of the test results:

Relationships	`twitter` **and** `revenues`	`facebook` **and** `revenues`
t	3.6516	9.2308
p-value	0.0003467	2.2e-16
correlation	0.2696854	0.5778213
Significant?	Yes	Yes

These results show that both pairs are positively correlated and the correlations are significant. It looks as if Bike Sharing LLC has found some good marketing channels linked to revenues. Does that mean advertising on these channels causes revenue to appear on the bottom line? Not necessarily.

There is a common misperception that correlation implies causation. Here is a fun look at two highly correlated variables:

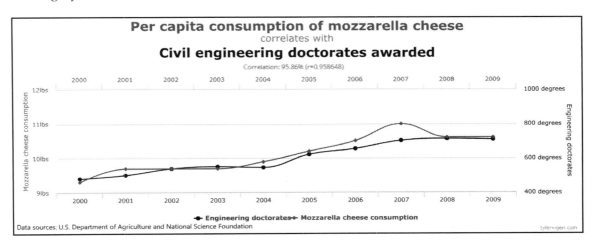

This is a correlation chart by Tyler Vigen (*2015*) available at http://tylervigen.com/spurious-correlations. This diagram is used under Creative Commons Attribution-International 4.0 Unported Licence (https://creativecommons.org/licenses/by/4./).

Wow! A correlation of 0.959. This makes you curious and you enter the data into R for a quick analysis. You have the skills to enter this data and verify it for yourself:

```
cheese <- c(9.3, 9.7, 9.7, 9.7, 9.9, 10.2, 10.5, 11, 10.6, 10.6)
degrees <- c(480, 501, 540, 552, 547, 622, 655, 701, 712, 708)
cor(cheese, degrees)
cor.test(cheese, degrees)
```

This verifies a correlation of `0.959`, as well as `t = 9.5274` and p-value of `1.217e-05`. Hmm? This correlation is strong, and it is significant! However, you know correlation does not imply causation. In fact, this chart (and many others like it) appear on the *Spurious Correlations* (*Vigen, 2015*) website to illustrate this point in a fun way:

> *"It is a condition of the human spirit to find the cause of phenomenon in order to explain it and answer questions. The pursuit is noble if the journey is sound."*
>
> *— Jay Gendron*

There are cases where the correlation is not significant. Running `cor.test()` on `google_adwords` and `facebook` results in an output showing no significance:

```
cor.test(marketing$google_adwords, marketing$facebook)
```

The output is as follows:

```
        Pearson's product-moment correlation
data:  marketing$google_adwords and marketing$facebook
t = 0.99948, df = 170, p-value = 0.319
alternative hypothesis: true correlation is not equal to 0
95 percent confidence interval:
 -0.07404915  0.22351032
sample estimates:
        cor
0.07643216
```

One last correlation test before you graphically explore some of these results. Your business sense wonders if there is any significant correlation between marketing expenditures (`marketing_total`) and `revenues` associated with marketing. This is a good business question that you can anticipate from the marketing group.

You run `cor.test(marketing$revenues, marketing$marketing_total)` and the results look promising: `correlation = 0.853`, `t = 21.313`, and `p-value = 2.2e-16`. The confidence interval is very tight (`0.806, 0.889`), indicating little variation in the data. A result like this suggests it is worth modeling this relationship in further analysis. You will generate a linear regression model on this pair of variables in `Chapter 4`, *Linear Regression for Business*.

Up to this point, you have been exploring correlation using tabular output. There is a role for graphical exploration as well. The following is the code to plot three bivariate correlations that you have already seen in the tabular form:

```
plot(marketing$google_adwords, marketing$revenues)
plot(marketing$google_adwords, marketing$facebook)
plot(marketing$marketing_total, marketing$revenues)
```

The output is shown in the following figure:

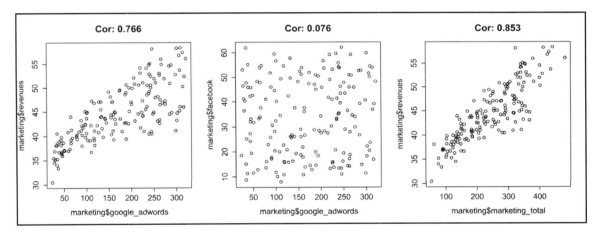

The plots reinforce the meaning behind the correlation values. Visually, you can see a relatively strong correlation in the left panel between `google_adwords` and `revenues`. The correlation is even stronger in the right panel between `revenues` and `marketing_total`. You know these correlations are significant as well.

The middle panel shows a random distribution of observations with no discernible pattern. This indicates a very weak relationship with a poor and insignificant correlation between the `google_adwords` and `facebook` variables.

This finishes analysis of two variables. Good work. It was a lot of material. Remember to remove the temporary `emp_factor` variable by running the following line of code presented earlier:

```
marketing$emp_factor <- NULL
```

Exploring multiple variables simultaneously

All right. You have arrived at the last section of exploratory data analysis. Now you will expand your exploration to multiple variables at once. Typical datasets have many variables, but a bivariate analysis limits you to pairwise comparisons. Exploring five variables, two at a time creates 10 pairs, 10 variables create 45, 20 variables create 190, 40 variables create 780, and so on. The impact on workflow is nearly exponential, as shown in the following diagram:

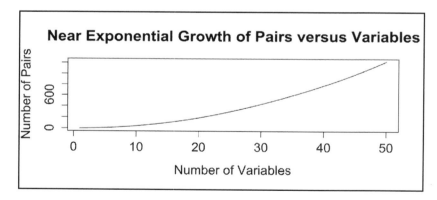

As the number of features (variables) in your dataset grows, your strategy for exploratory data analysis must scale along with your data. Your knowledge of bivariate exploratory data analysis provides you the following two benefits:

- You have the foundations for exploring multiple variables simultaneously
- You can use bivariate analysis to further explore any interesting pairs

You will still use the four-question approach of *Look-Relationships-Correlation-Significance*.

Look

The first question is, *what does the data look like?* You will use the same marketing dataset for this section, but this time, you will explore the entire dataset. Looking at the data is easily accomplished using the `summary()` function. Go ahead and look at the dataset again to refresh your memory of the 7 variables and 172 observations.

Relationships

Next, you want to know: *are there any relationship among the variables?* In the last section, you learned that the best way to do this is with graphical exploration. Wait a minute…we just said that plotting variables in pairs is very inefficient for many features. This is true. What if there was a way to plot all the pairs at once?

Go ahead and type `pairs(marketing)` into your console. Amazing! We will get the output as follows:

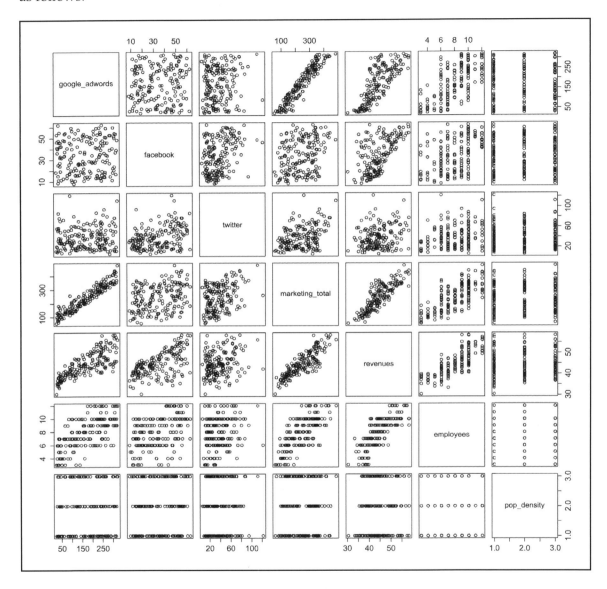

R tip: I have created pairs plots for 37 variables and it is amazing at what is visible in the thumbnails. You get quite a lot of information in very little code.

The output of `pairs(marketing)` is a grid of pairwise plots showing the relationship of each variable with the others. The diagonal of the grid helps you navigate the graphic and identify the pairs that you see. Here are two examples to show you the navigation:

- Revenues versus Google AdWords: Place your finger on the **google_adwords** panel at the left-hand top side. Move your finger four panels down to the row including **revenues**. This is the same plot you created in the last section and it shows a strong positive relationship.
- Facebook versus Google AdWords: Start with the **facebook** panel and move one panel to the left to the **google_adwords** column. This is the same plot you created in the last section and it shows nearly no relationship.

You now have a powerful and rapid visualization capability to find relationships.

Correlation

To find out *is there any correlation among the variables?*, you can use the `cor()` function in the dataset. Unlike the `pairs()` function, you can only find correlations between numeric variables. Subset marketing on the first six (numeric) variables and pass that to `cor()`:

```
cor(marketing[ ,1:6])
```

The output is as shown here:

	google_adwords	facebook	twitter	marketing_total	revenues	employees
google_adwords	1.00000000	0.07643216	0.0989750	0.9473566	0.7662461	0.6610312
facebook	0.07643216	1.00000000	0.3543410	0.3102232	0.5778213	0.4101966
twitter	0.09897500	0.35434096	1.0000000	0.3758691	0.2696854	0.2290618
marketing_total	0.94735659	0.31022316	0.3758691	1.0000000	0.8530354	0.7210171
revenues	0.76624608	0.57782131	0.2696854	0.8530354	1.0000000	0.7656857
employees	0.66103123	0.41019661	0.2290618	0.7210171	0.7656857	1.0000000

This function gives you insight about all pairwise correlations at once. Looking at the preceding console output, can you find the two correlations that you computed as pairs? Of course, you can. The following are the results of your earlier pairwise computations:

```
cor(marketing$google_adwords, marketing$revenues)
```

The output is as follows:

```
[1] 0.7662461
```

The second pair is shown in the following code:

```
cor(marketing$google_adwords, marketing$facebook)
```

The output is as follows:

```
[1] 0.07643216
```

Significance

Exploratory data analysis proceeds a bit more quickly when you explore multiple variables. You also see that the foundations learned in the last section allow you to find features and relationships of interest rapidly. The last question you have for this dataset before beginning to model is: *are there significant correlations in the data?*

At this point, you may not be surprised to learn that there is a way to run all correlation significance tests at once. The psych package provides a corr.test() function that combines the output of cor() along with the p-values. Review the *Is the correlation significant?* section if you need to solidify any of these concepts:

```
library(psych)
corr.test (marketing[ ,1:6])
```

The output is as follows:

```
Call:corr.test(x = marketing[, 1:6])
Correlation matrix
               google_adwords facebook twitter marketing_total revenues employees
google_adwords           1.00     0.08    0.10            0.95     0.77      0.66
facebook                 0.08     1.00    0.35            0.31     0.58      0.41
twitter                  0.10     0.35    1.00            0.38     0.27      0.23
marketing_total          0.95     0.31    0.38            1.00     0.85      0.72
revenues                 0.77     0.58    0.27            0.85     1.00      0.77
employees                0.66     0.41    0.23            0.72     0.77      1.00
Sample Size
[1] 172
Probability values (Entries above the diagonal are adjusted for multiple tests.)
               google_adwords facebook twitter marketing_total revenues employees
google_adwords           0.00     0.39    0.39               0        0      0.00
facebook                 0.32     0.00    0.00               0        0      0.00
twitter                  0.20     0.00    0.00               0        0      0.01
marketing_total          0.00     0.00    0.00               0        0      0.00
revenues                 0.00     0.00    0.00               0        0      0.00
employees                0.00     0.00    0.00               0        0      0.00
```

You can see that all the correlations in `Correlation matrix` are the same as the results when you called `cor()` in the marketing dataset. Additionally, the `corr.test()` function provides the probability values (p-values) for all pairs. While doing the bivariate analysis, you found results for some relationships. These compare well to the previous tabular output:

Relationship	Correlation	p-value	Significant?
`adwords` and `revenues`	0.76625	0.00	Yes
`facebook` and `revenues`	0.57782	0.00	Yes
`twitter` and `revenues`	0.26968	0.00	Yes
`adwords` and `facebook`	0.07643	0.319	No
`revenue` and `marketing_total`	0.853	0.00	Yes

You can also get insights about the entire dataset with graphical exploration. The `corrgram` package contains a `corrgram()` function, which is an enhanced version of the pairs plot and also incorporates elements of the `corr.test()` function.

Here is the code that produces a correlogram. It uses a subset of the marketing dataset because the mathematics only allows numeric values. `order` is set to `FALSE`, retaining the position of the variables as found in the dataset:

```
library(corrgram)
corrgram(marketing[ ,1:6], order = FALSE,
        main = "Correlogram of Marketing Data, Unordered",
        lower.panel = panel.conf, upper.panel = panel.ellipse,
        diag.panel = panel.minmax, text.panel = panel.txt)
```

Four parameters appear in the code. They control the content of the regions of the correlogram. These parameters in this example are explained as follows:

- **Lower Panel**: The bottom-left half of the graphic was set to display correlation coefficients and confidence intervals using `panel.conf`
- **Upper Panel**: The upper-right half of the graphic was set to display ellipses and smooth lines using `panel.ellipse`
- **Diagonal and Text**: The diagonal contains the name of the variable and its minimum and maximum values using `panel.minmax` and `panel.txt`, respectively

You can learn more about these parameters and other options by typing `?corrgram()` in the console and viewing the help available within the R environment.

Here is what the `corrgram()` function outputs:

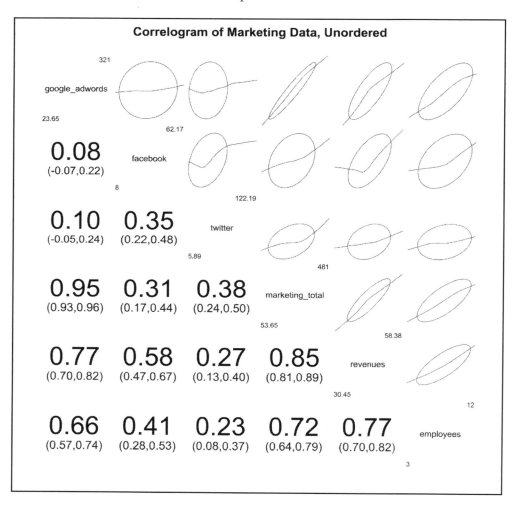

This single graphic incorporates a lot of information that you have seen with other functions. The following is an explanation of three key features of the correlogram:

- **Variables**: The variables appear along the diagonal with the minimum and maximum values of each.
- **Ellipses and Line**: The upper panel (top right) was coded to show confidence ellipses of each pair of variables. The ellipse captures the essential shape of the correlation scatterplot using a confidence interval, as well as a smooth line representation of the relationship between the two variables:
  - Skinny ellipses represent strong correlation
  - Rounder ellipses represent weak correlations
  - The slope of the smooth line represents positive or negative correlation
- **Correlation coefficient and confidence interval**: The lower panel (bottom left) was coded to show the correlation coefficient and confidence interval. This is similar to results you get from the `cor()` or `corr.test()` function.

 Learn more: The CRAN open source project has a good document that shows various examples of correlograms using different combinations of the function parameters. You can find the document (Wright, 2016) at `https://cran.r-project.org/web/packages/corrgram/vignettes/corrgram_examples.html`.

If you like to tailor the visuals to your audience, you can adjust the parameters. This time `order` is set to `TRUE`. This reorders the variables to present the strongest correlations towards the top left, with gradually weakening correlation towards the bottom right. Different parameters sent to the function result in a different graphic, as follows:

```
corrgram(marketing[ ,1:6], order = TRUE,
        main = "Correlogram of Marketing Data, Ordered",
        lower.panel = panel.shade, upper.panel = panel.pie,
        diag.panel = panel.minmax, text.panel = panel.txt)
```

The output is shown in the following figure:

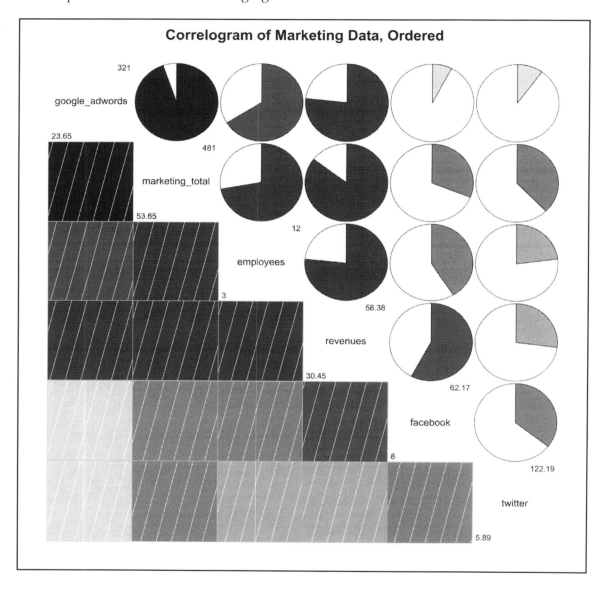

Further practice: Go back and explore the dataset you wrote to a file in
Chapter 2, *Data Cleaning*, and answer the following questions. As you are
reading this data from a file, the ordered factors and date formatting will
be lost. You already created the code in the last chapter. You can use it
again to convert variables into the correct data types:

```
bike <-
read.csv("./data/Ch2_clean_bike_sharing_data.csv",
                stringsAsFactors = TRUE)
bike$season <- factor(bike$season, ordered = TRUE,
                    levels = c("spring","summer",
                                "fall","winter"))
bike$weather <- factor(bike$weather, ordered = TRUE,
                    levels = c("clr_part_cloud",
                                "mist_cloudy",
                                "lt_rain_snow",
                                "hvy_rain_snow"))
library(lubridate)
bike$datetime <- ymd_hms(bike$datetime)
```

Questions: Use your new skills to explore the data and answer these
questions:

- Were you able to load the data and reconvert the data types?
  How many variables are in the dataset? How many
  observations?
- How many observations are there for each season?
- What is the mean and standard deviation of the temp variable?
- Which variable is distributed nearly normally?
- Which variable is most left skewed and most right skewed?
- Which pair of variables has the greatest positive correlation and
  greatest negative correlation?
- Which variable(s) shows significant correlation?

Answers: Complete code solutions for these practice exercises are found at
the website at http://jgendron.github.io/com.packtpub.intro.r.bi/:

- There are 13 variables and 17,379 observations:

```
spring summer   fall winter
  4242    4409   4496   4232
```

- For the `temp` variable, mean = 20.37647 and standard deviation = 7.894801.
- The `temp` variable is the most normally distributed.
- The `workingday` variable is the most left skewed and `casual` is the most right skewed.
- Greatest positive correlation is `temp` and `atemp` (`correlation = 0.99`) and greatest negative correlation is `humidity` and `casual` (`correlation = -0.37`).
- All variables show significant correlation. This is due in part to the large sample size.

Summary

Well done, data adventurer. You explored a dataset pretty thoroughly. Exploratory data analysis is the preliminary analysis step as it gives you insights about the features or relationships that are best for modeling. You learned that exploratory data analysis has a structure-it is not a series of random plots. The structure begins from having general questions in mind and then becoming familiar with the data by addressing four structured questions: *Look-Relationships-Correlation-Significance*.

Look provides you a big-picture idea of what is in the data, what type of scales and data types are used, and verification the data is suitable. This question relies mostly on tabular output. **Relationships** may exist between variables, and graphical exploration is well suited to spot them. **Correlations** are ways to describe relationships numerically, using the sign and value of correlation coefficients. There are many ways to calculate and display them. **Significance** helps determine whether the correlations visible in tabular or graphical output are also significant and not due to random chance.

Now that you have a sense of some possible influential features, you can take this knowledge and build better models to predict the outcomes. That is what you will do in the next chapter using the marketing dataset.

4
Linear Regression for Business

Linear regression is a powerful tool that enables the business analyst to perform data analytics and business intelligence. **Linear regression** is a statistical technique to represent relationships between two or more variables using a linear equation. You can use linear regression to predict an outcome, given some input. This chapter covers five topics that will give you the skills to use this technique in your analyses:

- Understanding linear regression
- Checking model assumptions
- Using a simple linear regression
- Refining data for simple linear regression
- Introducing multiple linear regression

Together, these topics provide a building-block approach to not only teach you the skills to build linear models, but also shape your analytical thinking. Using this approach with other datasets will help you to keep practicing these skills.

Use case: The Marketing Dataset
The marketing manager has asked you to analyze marketing data to provide insights about how expenditure on various types of advertising affects bottom-line revenues. You will use the same marketing data that you explored in the last chapter, but the employees and pop_density variables are removed. The Ch4_marketing.csv file is available on the book's website at
http://jgendron.github.io/com.packtpub.intro.r.bi/.

The dataset contains information about online advertisements, total marketing expenditures, and revenue for 172 bicycle sharing marketing campaigns across the country. The data comes from an industry trend analysis report. All variables are in thousands of dollars. Your exploratory data analysis revealed the dataset is clean, so you can get straight to work. Get set, go!

Understanding linear regression

There are several reasons why linear regression continues to be useful and powerful for data analytics:

- Linear regression tends to work well on a wide variety of datasets
- Linear regression can address many business intelligence problems
- Linear regression provides a solid foundation on which you can learn more advanced and sophisticated prediction modeling techniques

In a business context, analysts use linear regression in diverse endeavors such as evaluating trends, making revenue estimates, analyzing the impact of price or supply changes, and assessing risk. You will start this journey by building a linear model.

The lm() function

The principal tool used for linear regression in R is the `lm()` function. Refer to its help page by typing `?lm` into your console. You will see the function has 13 arguments. For the most part, you will be using just two arguments, `formula` and `data`.

When you run a linear regression using `lm()`, R returns an object of the `lm` class. This object is actually an R list containing many different components. On the `lm()` help page, these components are listed under the **Value** section. Go ahead and look at this information as you will be using it in this chapter.

R tip: Pay close attention to the output of R functions. Read the **Value** section of the help pages carefully and try to understand the nature of the output. In particular, learn to understand complex output objects, such as lists and how to extract the individual components from them for use in analysis.

Start by loading the data into the `adverts` variable. By using the `str()` function that you learned in `Chapter 2`, *Data Cleaning*, you will see that this dataset consists of 172 observations:

```
adverts <- read.csv("./data/Ch4_marketing.csv"); str(adverts)
```

Each observation has five variables that provide expenditures on three different advertising methods, total marketing cost, and revenue.

By using the `pairs()` function that you learned in `Chapter 3`, *Exploratory Data Analysis*, you will notice a very strong correlation between the `marketing_total` and `revenues` variables. Create a scatterplot to look at this relationship more closely:

```
pairs(adverts)
plot(adverts$marketing_total, adverts$revenues, ylab = "Revenues",
     xlab = "Marketing Total", main = "Revenues and Marketing")
```

We will get a pairs plot and scatterplot as follows:

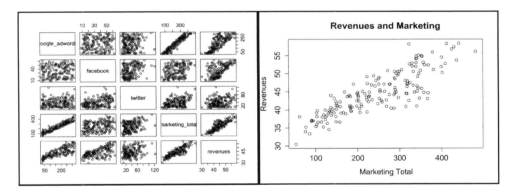

It is easy to imagine a straight line extending from the lower-left of the scatterplot to the upper-right, running straight through the data. This is a primary indication that the relationship might lend itself to linear regression.

BI tip: Regression analysis is a key tool in any analyst's toolbox. A common use is determining the effects of a price increase on demand for products. It provides leaders with an interpretable relationship of how one input affects another.

Simple linear regression

You run an **simple linear regression** (**SLR**) by formulating a model with your data. The formulation generally consists of a response variable (Y) and a predictor variable (X), linked by a tilda (~). You can think of this formulation as either *Y as a function of X* or *Y regressed on X*. The data needs to be in a data frame. A generic example in R would look similar to the following:

```
model <- lm(Y ~ X, data = dataset)
```

It is now time for you to build an SLR. The first line of the code runs the regression and saves the lm object to a variable called model1. The second line displays the contents of the model1 object to the console:

```
model1 <- lm(revenues ~ marketing_total, data = adverts)
model1
```

The output is as follows:

```
Call:
lm(formula = revenues ~ marketing_total, data = adverts)

Coefficients:
    (Intercept)   marketing_total
       32.00670           0.05193
```

This output informs you about the following two things:

- Call summarizes the model. It reminds you that you are using the lm() model, the formulation used (revenues ~ marketing_total), and the adverts dataset.
- Coefficients provides you with two important numbers: an Intercept of 32.00670, and a slope (marketing_total) with a value of 0.05193.

Interpreting your models: Models are full of numbers. Without the ability to interpret them, they provide little use to business leaders. In the case of your first SLR, you will articulate the output using the following statements:

- Revenue increases by $51.93 for every $1,000 increase in total marketing
- Revenue is $32,007 when total marketing expenditure is $0

The `Intercept` value is important for model execution, but may not have as much interpretability. In your case, this number sets the baseline level for the model.

The intercept and slope provide the parameters for a prediction equation:

Revenue = 32.0067 + (0.05193 * marketing_total)

Before we continue, you should take a quick detour to learn about **residuals**, the variation between the model and reality.

Residuals

Residuals play an important role in linear models. Statistics play a crucial role in understanding and minimizing residuals. What exactly is a residual? Look at your data again, but this time with the regression line and a few other markers added:

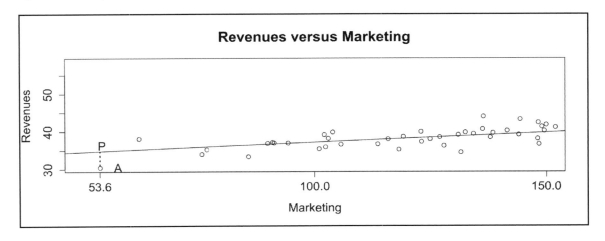

For every value of **Marketing**, there are two values of Revenues associated with it:

- **Actual value** of `revenues`: You will find this value in the dataset. The letter **A** (for **Actual**) in the lower left-hand corner of the plot designates one such value. For instance, when *Marketing = 53.6*, the *actual* corresponding value of *Revenues* is 30.45.
- **Predicted value** of `revenues`: This is the *predicted* value of *Revenues* found on the regression line, when *Marketing = 53.6*. We know, from our prediction formula, that this is *32 + (0.05 * 53.6) = 34.68*, shown as **P** (for **Predicted**).

The residual (or error term) is the difference between the predicted value of Revenues (34.68) and the actual value of Revenues (30.45), when Marketing is 53.6. The dotted line on the plot highlights this difference:

residual = Predicted Value – Actual Value = 34.68 – 30.45 = 4.23

There are 172 observations in the dataset. Therefore, there will be 172 residuals in the SLR model. There is a lot more to learn about residuals. For now, you know enough to understand how to check the assumptions of SLR modeling.

Checking model assumptions

To use linear regression, your data must satisfy the following four core assumptions:

- Linearity
- Independence
- Normality
- Equal variance

It may be helpful to think of these assumptions by their first letters. You can remember that **LINE** is an important aspect of linear regression. Next, you will learn about each of the assumptions as well as tests that you can perform in R to check whether the data satisfies them.

Learn more: Checking the assumptions of a statistical model is important. The power and accuracy of any model comes from its adherence to the assumptions. David Robinson (*2015*) has written a blog called **VARIANCE EXPLAINED** that describes this topic in an enjoyable way:
`http://varianceexplained.org/r/kmeans-free-lunch/`

Linearity

Linearity assumption: The relationship between the predictor and response variables is linear.

In an SLR situation, a quick way to determine linearity is to plot the variables with a scatterplot. Earlier, you saw a strong correlation and linearity between the `marketing_total` and `revenues` variables. A straight line would run through the data. This appears to meet the linearity assumption. Things get more complex when using more than one predictor variable, but you can see this assumption more easily when plotting only one predictor variable.

Independence

Independence assumption: The relationship between variables is independent of one another.

This is probably the most difficult assumption to test. You can typically handle it using common sense along with an understanding of the data and its collection method. A good example of independence is observations in the marketing data. They all come from a different location. It is reasonable to assume that the marketing budgets from one location have no impact on another.

Here is an example of data that would probably not meet the independence assumption. Consider a dataset with variables such as income, age, and occupation. As you may imagine, there is probably some dependence between income and a person's age or occupation. Another thing to watch for is whether the data is time based. Then, an observation is dependent on the one(s) before it. These are time series data. You will analyze them using a different technique that you will learn in `Chapter 6`, *Time Series Analysis*.

Normality

Normality assumption: The residuals form a normal distribution around the regression line with a mean value of zero.

A histogram provides an excellent way to view the distribution of the residuals. Another plot to check the normality is the normal quantile, or Q-Q, plot created using the `qqnorm()` function. It tests for normality by plotting the data by quantiles, comparing how they actually appear versus how they would appear in a theoretical normal plot.

The following code creates a two-panel plot with a histogram in the left panel and the Q-Q plot in the right. The `$` operator is used to extract the residuals from the `model1` object:

```
par(mfrow = c(1, 2))
hist(model1$residuals, xlab = "Residuals", col = "gray",
     main = "Residuals Distribution")
qqnorm(model1$residuals, main = "Q-Q Plot of Residuals")
qqline(model1$residuals)
```

The histogram shows residuals that look normally distributed. Meanwhile, the closer the residuals hug the diagonal line in the Q-Q plot, the more normal the distribution, as shown in the following diagrams:

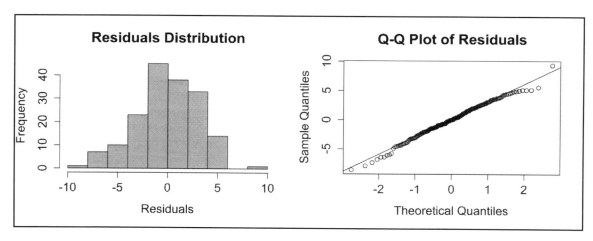

Notice what looks like a small outlier on the right edge of the histogram. The quirk in the upper-right corner of the Q-Q plot corresponds to this possible outlier in the histogram. You will learn more about outliers at the end of this chapter.

Equal variance

Equal variance assumption: Residuals form a random pattern distributed around a mean of zero.

You can see this by plotting the residuals against the fitted (predicted) values of the model:

```
plot(model1$fitted.values, model1$residuals, ylab = "Residuals",
    xlab = "Fitted Values", main="Residuals Distribution")
abline(0, 0, lwd = 3); abline(h = c(-6.5, 6.5), lwd = 3, lty = 3)
```

The code once again uses the $ operator to extract the residuals. It is also extracts the fitted values from model1. The abline() function was used to create reference lines of a mean around zero and for a visual indictor of equal variance:

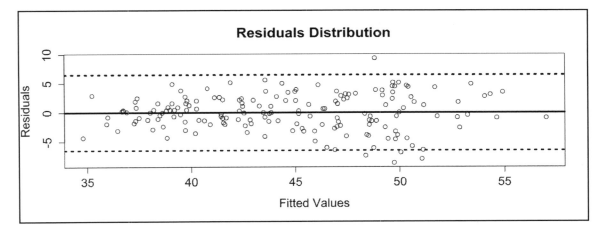

When inspecting a residuals plot for equal variance, you look for the following two things:

- You *DO* want to see the residuals randomly distributed in a tubular pattern, indicated by the dotted lines
- You *DO NOT* want residuals with a pattern that looks similar to a fan or funnel, or in some way curvilinear

The residuals in this plot are pretty close to being equally distributed.

Assumption wrap-up

"A rule of thumb is that if things look OK, then they probably are OK."

– Anonymous

You built a simple model. Modeling is easy, but it requires skill to know that it is appropriate for the data. Notice the amount of time you spent making sure the model met the assumptions of linear regression. Some assumptions are more important than others, as follows:

- All linear regression operations and results are very sensitive to even small departures from independence.
- All operations are sensitive to moderate departures from equal variance.
- Some operations deal well with departures from normality. One exception is that prediction intervals are quite sensitive to departures from normality.

You will later discuss how to transform data when it does not meet the assumptions.

Using a simple linear regression

You built a linear regression model by simply using the `lm()` function on your data. You also used the LINE approach to make sure that your model satisfied the assumptions of linear regression. Building SLRs is often straightforward, but it is very important that you know how to interpret the output.

Interpreting model output

There is a lot of information available within a linear regression model. You can see an expanded output by using the `summary()` function:

```
summary(model1)
```

The following is the output:

```
Call:
lm(formula = revenues ~ marketing_total, data = adverts)

 Residuals:
    Min      1Q  Median      3Q     Max
-8.6197 -1.8963 -0.0006  2.1705  9.3689
```

```
Coefficients:
                Estimate Std. Error t value Pr(>|t|)
(Intercept)     32.006696   0.635590   50.36   <2e-16 ***
marketing_total  0.051929   0.002437   21.31   <2e-16 ***
---
Signif. codes:  0 '***' 0.001 '**' 0.01 '*' 0.05 '.' 0.1 ' ' 1

Residual standard error: 3.054 on 170 degrees of freedom
Multiple R-squared:  0.7277,  Adjusted R-squared:  0.7261
F-statistic: 454.2 on 1 and 170 DF,  p-value: < 2.2e-16
```

R tip: This is a good time to review the help available for the `lm()` function. Type `?lm` into your console and read the section on `Value`.

The summary output has the following important components:

- `Residuals` provide the Tukey five-number summary of the residuals (you learned this in `Chapter 3`, *Exploratory Data Analysis*). This particular output is consistent with what you saw in your residual analysis, namely that the residuals distribution is relatively normal around a mean of zero.

- `Coefficients` are the same as you saw before, but now you also see the standard errors, t-values, and p-values. Recall the concept of the null hypothesis from `Chapter 3`, *Exploratory Data Analysis*. The p-value is a measure of how surprised you would be to see the result in the null hypothesis that the intercept and slope equal zero. The p-value in each case is substantially less than the statistical benchmark of 0.05, meaning that if either of them were zero, you would be very surprised at this result.

- `Adjusted R-squared` tells you how much error your model explains. In this case, your model accounts for nearly 73% of the error. The goodness of this sort of percentage varies from domain to domain.

- `F-statistic` (and its associated `p-value`) indicate whether your overall model works. In the case of SLR, with a single predictor, the `p-value` associated with the slope is sufficient for this. `F-statistic` is more useful with **multiple linear regression (MLR)**.

Learn more: If you need a refresher about the null hypothesis and hypothesis testing, you can learn more online at Stat Trek or Khan Academy:
http://stattrek.com/hypothesis-test/hypothesis-testing.aspx
https://www.khanacademy.org/math/probability/statistics-infere
ntial/hypothesis-testing/v/hypothesis-testing-and-p-values

You have a lot of information about your data now. So what can you do? One thing you can do is make predictions.

Predicting unknown outputs with an SLR

You can predict outputs using your SLR model. This works best if you predict using inputs inside the range of your existing model. In the marketing dataset, you can predict revenues within `range(adverts$marketing_total)`, which is $[53.65, 481.0]$.

 Extrapolation woes: You can predict responses outside the range of your input variables; however, you do not have as much confidence in how the model behaves outside the range of data you have. Perhaps the response becomes exponential at an input of 550. This would result in bad predictions.

Suppose you want to predict revenues if you spend $460,000 in marketing. The data does not have an input of 460. You can see this using the `select()` and `filter()` functions:

```
library(dplyr)
select(adverts, marketing_total) %>% filter(marketing_total > 430)
```

The output is shown here:

```
  marketing_total
1          481.00
2          435.49
3          440.94
```

This non-sorted, quick look shows a gap in the data between `440.94` and the maximum value, `481.00`. There is simply nothing there. The `predict.lm()` function allows you to estimate outputs based on other inputs. You will pass the `predict.lm()` function a new input, typically held in a data frame called `newdata`, as well as a `predict` interval:

```
newdata <- data.frame(marketing_total = 460)
predict.lm(model1, newdata, interval = "predict")
```

It will return the output as follows:

```
        fit      lwr      upr
1 55.89403 49.75781 62.03025
```

The `predict.lm()` output tells you that, for an input value of $460,000, the estimated revenue is $55,894. Keep in mind, this is only an estimate; you cannot really predict the future. Every estimate has a degree of uncertainty, but R allows you to quantify the uncertainty by providing a **confidence interval (CI)**.

 Confidence intervals: The default prediction CI is 95%. You can understand a 95% CI by imagining that, if you were to make 100 predictions using `marketing_total` equal to 460, then 95 outputs would fall in the range of 49.75781 to 62.03025.

Suppose you want a tighter 99% CI. Changing the CI in your prediction is easy to do. Change the default parameter by passing `level = 0.99`:

```
predict.lm(model1, newdata, level = 0.99, interval = "predict")
```

The output is as follows:

```
          fit      lwr      upr
1  55.89403 47.79622 63.99184
```

Notice the CI got bigger. Can you figure out why? If you want to be more confident, then you have to allow for more uncertainty in the prediction. If you only needed 90% confidence, you would find more certain results: `lwr = 50.753` and `upr = 61.03506`.

You can also use `predict.lm()` to examine multiple input values of `marketing_total`:

```
newdata = data.frame(marketing_total = c(450, 460, 470))
predict.lm(model1, newdata, interval = "predict")
```

The following is the output:

```
          fit      lwr      upr
1  55.37474 49.24653 61.50295
2  55.89403 49.75781 62.03025
3  56.41332 50.26873 62.55791
```

In each case, you get the estimated value, along with a 95% confidence interval.

Working with big data using confidence intervals

You will find the term *big data* used in different ways. One definition is *a dataset that is too big for processing given current techniques or hardware* (*Sicular*, *2013*). Computer scientists have dealt with big data by developing algorithms, such as MapReduce, and frameworks, such as Hadoop. These distribute the data to multiple processors where they bin and count data by category (Map) and then assemble the various outputs into an aggregated result (Reduce).

Statisticians, on the other hand, developed sampling techniques as one way of dealing with similar problems. Imagine that you have a dataset with billions of observations, and that processing such a dataset on your machine would take too long. Under certain conditions, you might take smaller samples of this data, process these samples, and then try to infer things about the larger dataset.

 Learn more: Big data is not a new phenomenon. The issue of large dataset's exceeding capabilities actually goes back centuries. Refer to John Rauser's (*2011*) 17-minute YouTube video, What is a Career in Big Data? at `https://www.youtube.com/watch?v=0tuEEnL61HM`.

When you use a sample from a larger population, you cannot be certain that your model output is correct. It is just an estimate of some unknown true parameter associated with the larger population. Like predictions, confidence intervals can help mitigate this problem. For example, take a random sample of 30% of your marketing data:

```
set.seed(4510)
market_sample <- sample_frac(adverts, 0.30, replace = FALSE)
```

Set a randomization seed to allow you to get repeatable results. Then use the `sample_frac()` function from the `dplyr` library. You can pass a fraction as a parameter. Setting `replace = FALSE` pulls samples without putting them back. Then run `lm()`:

```
samp_model <- lm(revenues ~ marketing_total, data = market_sample)
samp_model
```

The output is as follows:

```
Call:
lm(formula = revenues ~ marketing_total, data = market_sample)
Coefficients:
    (Intercept)   marketing_total
       31.08243           0.05531
```

The coefficients for the `Intercept` and `marketing_total` are close to the values you saw in `model1`, but not quite the same. If you were to take a different sample, then you would get slightly different coefficients again. You can use the `confint()` function to gain insights about population estimates while accounting for sampling uncertainty:

```
confint(samp_model)
```

The output is shown here:

```
                     2.5 %         97.5 %
  (Intercept)      28.49785446  33.66700509
  marketing_total   0.04615628   0.06445785
```

What this shows is that if you take 100 different random samples from the population, then 95 of the 100 samples would estimate the slope of `marketing_total` between the values `0.04615628` and `0.06445785`. Indeed, the slope of `marketing_total` in the marketing dataset is `0.05193`, which falls in this interval. You now have a tool that can help you analyze a big data dataset and have some confidence in the estimates you calculate.

Refining data for simple linear regression

As discussed earlier, there may be times when your diagnostic plots indicate that the data does not meet all the assumptions specified by the LINE approach (Linearity, Independence, Normality, and Equal variance).

Consider the following simple dataset. Run a SLR and generate its diagnostic plots:

```
x0 <- c(1, 2, 3, 4, 5, 6, 7, 8, 9, 10)
y0 <- c(1.00, 1.41, 1.73, 2.00, 2.24,
        2.45, 2.65, 2.83, 3.00, 3.16)
fit0 <- lm(y0 ~ x0)

par(mfrow = c(1, 3))
plot(x0, y0, pch = 19, main = "Linearity?"); abline(fit0)
hist(fit0$residuals, main = "Normality?", col = "gray")
plot(fit0$fitted.values, fit0$residuals,
     main = "Equal Variance?", pch = 19); abline(h = 0)
```

The diagnostic plots generated are as follows:

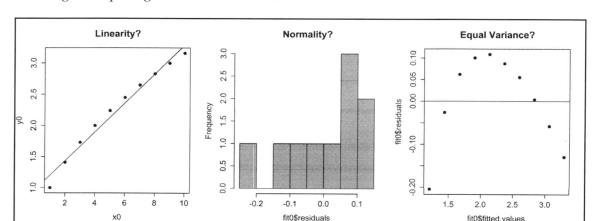

The first plot shows some deviation from linearity. Recall the saying *If things look OK, then they probably are OK*. You are going to focus on the other two plots, which do not meet the assumptions of normality or equal variance. We simulated the data, so we can tell you the secret to fixing this data. Specifically, the values of the y0 variable are the square roots of the x0 variable. It is often possible to transform the data mathematically. This results in a dataset that satisfies the necessary assumptions of linear regression.

Transforming data

A transformation is an operation to fix data so that it meets model needs. In order to run an SLR, data should satisfy the LINE assumptions. There are some general rules of thumb available to you depending on the assumption(s) that the data fails to satisfy:

- **Not independent**: You may need to transform your independent variables into a time series and apply a time series analysis. This approach is in Chapter 6, *Time Series Analysis*.
- **Not linear**: You might consider transforming the independent (input) variable.
- **Not normal or unequal variance**: You might consider transforming the response variable (the dependent variable).

You can fix this simulated dataset by squaring the y0 variable using the ^2 operator. The transformed variable is stored as y0_t:

```
y0_t <- y0^2
fit0_t <- lm(y0_t ~ x0)

plot(x0, y0_t, pch = 19, main = "Linear"); abline(fit0_t)
hist(fit0_t$residuals, main = "Normal", col = "gray")
plot(fit0_t$fitted.values, fit0_t$residuals,
    main = "Equal Variance", pch = 19); abline(h = 0)
```

The output is shown as follows:

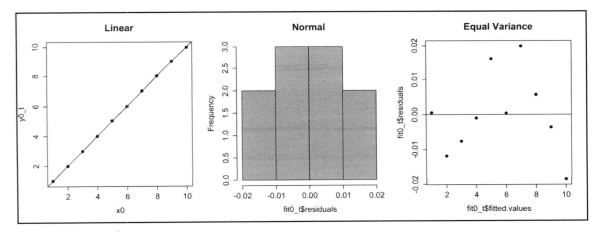

You transformed the dependent variable. Now, both the histogram and the plot of residuals versus fitted values show that the data meets the assumptions of normality and equal variance. The scatterplot to the left now reveals that the transformed variable, y0_t, behaves more linearly. Transforming variables is a common method to satisfy assumptions. Thankfully, the R software provides a useful library called MASS to help you transform your data. The boxcox() function will help identify possible transformations. Load the library and then run the function against your original, untransformed SLR-fitted model object:

```
library(MASS)
boxcox(fit0)
```

The following is the output:

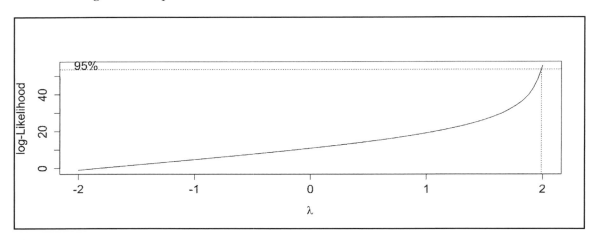

The graphical output gives you a clue about the exponent to which you will raise your response variable. The level of lambda (λ̂) is **2**, as shown by the vertical dotted line. This is just what you did. You raised the y0 variable to the second power to get the fit you needed.

Now, consider an example of transforming independent (input) variables. Here are some new data and diagnostic plots:

```
x1 <- c(1, 5, 15, 30, 60, 120, 240, 480,
        720, 1440, 2880, 5760, 10080)
y1 <- c(0.84, 0.71, 0.61, 0.56, 0.54, 0.47,
        0.45, 0.38, 0.36, 0.26, 0.2, 0.16, 0.08)
fit1 <- lm(y1 ~ x1)

plot(x1, y1, pch = 19, main = "Linearity?"); abline(fit1)
hist(fit1$residuals, main = "Normality?", col = "gray")
plot(fit1$fitted.values, fit1$residuals,
     main = "Equal Variance?", pch = 19); abline(h = 0)
```

The diagnostic plots generated are as follows:

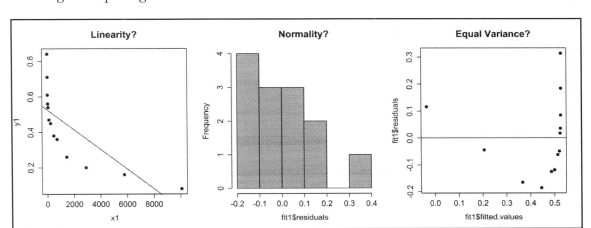

These plots show problems with the assumptions to include severe non-linearity. The rules of thumb indicate that you might consider transforming the independent variable when working with non-linear data. Unfortunately, the `boxcox()` function does not work with independent variables. If you do run this function, you will get a lambda (λ) ranging from -1.2 to -0.7. You can try transforming the response variable by raising y0 to the power of -1.0, but it does not solve the linearity problem. This is because the problem is with the independent variable. How will you transform the independent variable?

Look at the logarithmic pattern in the scatterplot. A good place to start is often with a `log()` transformation, that is to say, transforming the independent variable by the natural logarithm function and then performing the regression:

```
x1_t <- log(x1)
fit1_t <- lm(y1 ~ x1_t)

plot(x1_t, y1, pch = 19, main = "Linear"); abline(fit1_t)
hist(fit1_t$residuals, main = "Normal", col = "gray")
plot(fit1_t$fitted.values, fit1_t$residuals,
     main = "Equal Variance", pch = 19); abline(h = 0)
```

Transforming the independent variable handles the nonlinearity. Now the data meets the other assumptions as well. Data transformations are a complex topic. There may be times when the rules of thumb are not sophisticated enough to help you or when the independent and response variables need transformations:

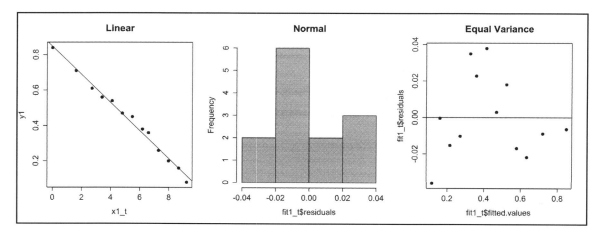

You will learn transformations by experience and research. Often you will need to experiment with different combinations of transformations to arrive at the right solution.

Handling outliers and influential points

An outlier is a data point that does not follow the trend of the response variables. You handle outliers by dealing with the individual data points rather than transforming the dataset mathematically. Consider this data and inspect the plots. Can you see the outliers?

```
x2 <- 1:20
y2 <- c(1:10, 4, 12:20)
x3 <- c(1:20, 30)
y3 <- c(0.4, 2.2, 2.2, 5.6, 5.3, 5.2, 7.5, 8.7, 9.6, 9.7, 12.5,
        12.4, 12.4, 11.8, 16.1, 16, 17, 18.9, 19.8, 20.6, 30.0)
```

The plots are shown here:

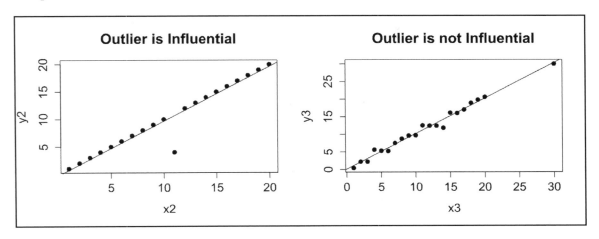

If you noticed two outliers (x2, y2) = (11, 4) and (x3, y3) = (30, 30), then you are correct. The next question is, *Why is the first outlier influential while the second is not?* An **influential point** is an outlier that disproportionately alters the result of a regression model. The influence could affect the predicted responses, the estimates of the slope coefficients, or the results of the hypothesis test(s).

If you run an SLR on the first dataset, you will see the results change by removing the influential outlier. This is because the outlier broke the general trend of an increasing response. Can you see how it lies below all the other points in the trend? The influential outliner has pulled the predictive line down. Conversely, if you remove the outlier in the second dataset, you will find a subtle change in the output, but it is not exceptional. You see that the outlier follows the general trend of the response values:

Practice: Load the data in the following code into R and determine whether there is an outlier. If an outlier exists, is it influential? Use a scatterplot to assist you. Include the fitted regression line in the plot.

```
x4 <- c(1:20)
y4 <- c(0.4, 2.2, 2.2, 5.6, 5.3, 5.2, 7.5, 8.7,
        9.6, 9.7, 12.5, 12.4, 12.4, 12.8, 16.1,
        16.0, 17.0, 11.5, 19.8, 20.6)
```

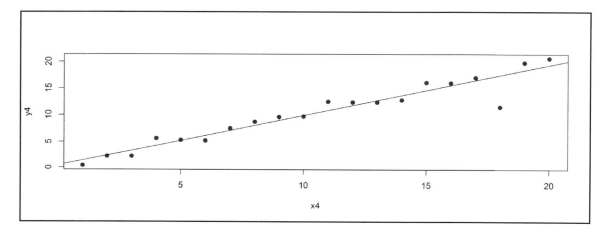

The data point at (x4, y4) = (18, 11.5) is an outlier, and it is probably an influential point. Try doing regression on the dataset with this point included in the dataset, and then with this point removed. Compare the regression outputs. Is the outlier affecting the results? According to the summary table of the regression output, the outlier is influencing the results:

Regression output	With outlier	Without outlier
Residual (min, median, max)	(-5.94, 0.43, 1.65)	(-1.49, 0.15, 1.51)
Intercept and slope	0.4805, 0.9423	0.0107, 1.0200
Adjusted R-squared	0.9151	0.9821
F-Statistic	205.7	986.1

So how do you identify outliers and influential points? A very good way to spot outliers is visually. In `Chapter 3`, *Exploratory Data Analysis*, you learned about boxplots, histograms, and scatterplots. These simple tools help reveal patterns and anomalies in your data. Identifying influential points is a bit trickier, but there is an analytic tool called **Cook's Distance** to help you. How do you find Cook's Distance? Use the `plot()` function on the model object.

R tip: You do not need to learn the theory or mathematics of Cook's Distance to use it. The following is a rule of thumb you can apply to outliers:

- **Suspicious**: If a data point has a Cook's Distance > 0.5
- **Likely influential**: If a data point has a Cook's Distance > 1.0
- **Influential**: If a point has a Cook's Distance that stands out from all the others

Run the `plot({model_name})` function on the practice problem data, including the outlier. This will produce four plots. The first two plots provide information similar to that generated when checking model assumptions: **Residuals vs Fitted**, and **Normal Q-Q**. The third plot (**Scale-Location**) is beyond the scope of this book. The fourth plot, **Residuals vs Leverage**, provides Cook's Distance.

You can see the dotted lines in the lower part of the bottom-right panel indicating the rings of Cook's Distance equal to **0.5** and **1.0**. Given the dataset (x4, y4), you can see that the 18th data point in the dataset is outside the Cook's Distance rings. Using the rule of thumb, it is not only greater than 1.0, but it also stands out from the other data points. Therefore, data point 18 is a cause for concern. What can you do to refine the data?

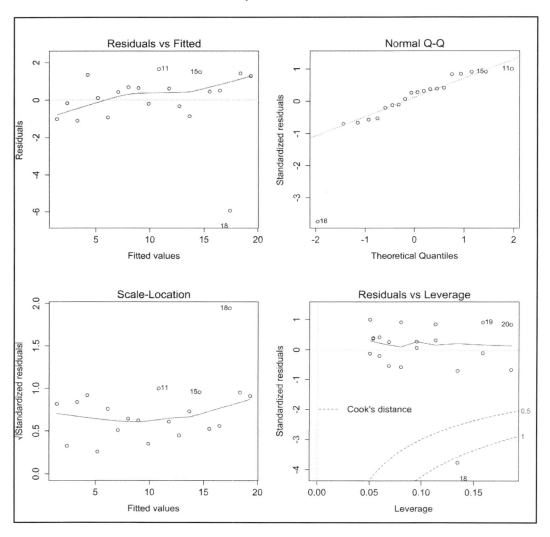

Here is a summary of the steps you can keep in mind when dealing with problematic data points:

- **Errors**: Begin by using exploratory data analysis to see if there are errors in the data. This is common and it could solve the problem.
- **Recheck assumptions**: Maybe there are non-linearity issues after all. If this is the case, you might have to change the type of model used.
- **Incorrect formulation**: There is the possibility that you did not properly formulate your regression model. Consider other formulations.
- **Delete data points**: As a last resort, consider deleting data points. Be advised that this is both controversial and potentially hazardous to your results. You should have a very good reason for deleting data. Do not remove data just because the regression model is not turning out the way you would like. If you do remove the data, make sure you describe it in your data analysis, and provide your justification for deleting it.

If everything else fails, do multiple analyses. Perform one linear regression with the outlier(s) and another without them. Include the results from both approaches in your final analysis. Use common sense and subject matter expertise. Do not be afraid to ask a more experienced analyst what they think.

 R tip: Spotting and dealing with outliers and influential data points is not simple. There can be a lot of subjectivity involved, and subject matter expertise may be required.

Introducing multiple linear regression

It is time to introduce you to the topic of MLR. In SLR, you will use a single predictor variable. Most business problems deal with outputs dependent on more than two input variables. MLR is the technique used for situations having two or more predictor variables.

In the *Using a simple linear regression* section, you looked at revenue as a function of the marketing budget. You learned a great deal about the relationship by regressing the `revenues` variable on the `marketing_total` variable.

The total amount spent on marketing is the sum of `google_adwords`, `facebook`, and `twitter` marketing expenditures. Using MLR, you can examine the relationship among revenue and some or all of these component budgets.

You will formulate an MLR similar to an SLR, but with more predictor terms. You can think of this formulation as *Y regressed on X1 and X2 and so forth*. The most common relationship is an additive relationship, and the + operator is used to include multiple variables. The data needs to be in a data frame. A generic example in R would look similar to the following:

```
model <- lm(Y ~ X1 + X2 + ..., data = dataset)
```

Here is the formulation after you model the revenue regressed on all three components of the marketing budget:

```
model2 <- lm(revenues ~ google_adwords + facebook + twitter,
             data = adverts)
```

As you learned with SLR modeling, you will want to verify that the data meets the assumptions of LINE. Do this before continuing with model interpretation or reporting.

Instead of creating individual plots as you did for SLR, you have learned the `plot()` function. You can run it on the fitted model by running `plot(model2)`:

- Look at linearity and equal variance from the **Residuals vs Fitted** plot
- Think about independence based on the data source and its collection
- Assess the normality assumption with the **Normal Q-Q** plot
- Identify outliers that are influential with the **Residuals vs Leverage** plot

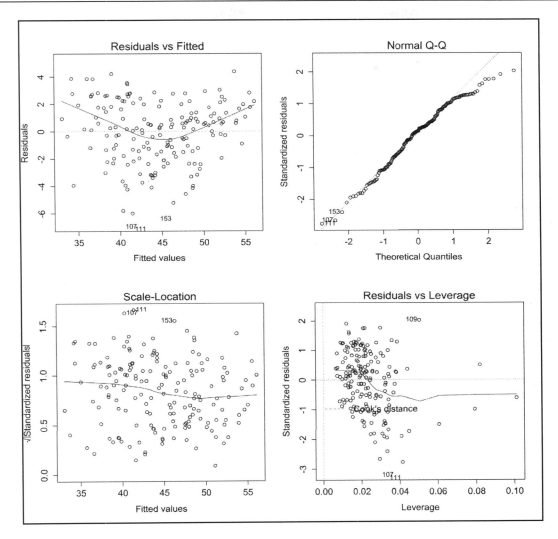

You will see that the **Residuals vs Fitted** plot shows a slight bow, which might indicate non-linearity. You could experiment with your transformation skills and see if you can come up with something better. Running `summary(model2)` provides this output for interpretation. Use what you learned when interpreting SLR output:

```
Call:
lm(formula = revenues ~ google_adwords + facebook + twitter,
    data = adverts)
Residuals:
    Min     1Q   Median     3Q      Max
```

```
-5.9971 -1.4566  0.2791  1.7428  4.3711
Coefficients:
               Estimate Std. Error t value Pr(>|t|)
(Intercept)    29.545988  0.533523   55.38  <2e-16 ***
google_adwords  0.048384  0.001947   24.85  <2e-16 ***
facebook        0.197651  0.011871   16.65  <2e-16 ***
twitter         0.003889  0.008270    0.47   0.639
---
Signif. codes:  0 '***' 0.001 '**' 0.01 '*' 0.05 '.' 0.1 ' ' 1
Residual standard error: 2.214 on 168 degrees of freedom
Multiple R-squared:  0.8585,  Adjusted R-squared:  0.856
F-statistic: 339.8 on 3 and 168 DF,  p-value: < 2.2e-16
```

One of the first things you want to look at when you run an MLR is the `F-statistic` and its associated `p-value`. `F-statistic` tells you something about your null hypothesis. In an MLR, the null hypothesis is that all the coefficients are zero. Stated differently, the null hypothesis is that there is no relationship between the three predictors and the output, `revenues`.

In this case, the `p-value` is 2.2e-16. This is substantially lower than 0.05, which is the threshold where you generally reject the null hypothesis. In other words, with a p-value less than 0.05, you have strong evidence that there is, in fact, a relationship between the three predictors and `revenues`. OK, you know that this model tells you something about the relationship between the predictors and the response. However, what is it telling you?

The `Adjusted R-squared` value of `0.856` indicates the model explains over 85 percent of the variance in the data. This is a good explanation of fit. Now you know your model fits the data, and you know it explains a lot of the variance. You may want to know if you need all three predictors in the formulation, or can you do just as well with a subset?

The three predictors result in three coefficients as well as three individual p-values. You interpret them as you did for the overall model: low p-values indicate that the variable helps explain the model better than higher p-values. For instance, perhaps the `twitter` variable is unnecessary in the model given its very high p-value of `0.639`.

Learn more: This interpretation of this small MLR provides you with the insights to start exploring a useful tool. Many other questions emerge when working with an MLR, such as interactions among the predictors, collinearity among the predictors, and categorical variables in the predictors, to name but a few. You can learn more about this and other topics from a wide range of sources. Look at the textbook available online at http://www.statsoft.com/textbook/multiple-regression.

Summary

In this chapter, you examined a business scenario using SLR with one predictor variable and one response variable. You began by understanding the basic components of a simple linear regression including model formulation, inspection, interpretation, and diagnostics. You then learned how to determine whether the data met all the necessary assumptions for liner models, as well as how to use the model to predict outcomes and quantify your confidence in the results.

In situations where the data violated any assumptions, you learned how to transform the data using a structured approach. You also learned how to identify anomalous data known as outliers and determine whether they were influential points. Finally, you began to learn about models that have more than one predictor variable and required multiple linear regression.

In the next chapter, you will learn a different type of modeling called cluster analysis. It is useful for data that has very different characteristics and cannot be analyzed using linear regression.

5

Data Mining with Cluster Analysis

Data mining is a term that is been around since the 1990s. What exactly is data mining? Data mining is the process of working with a large amount of data to gather insights and detect patterns. Analysts often use it when the data does not include a response variable, yet there is a belief that a relationship or information about the structure of the data lies within it. This chapter will cover the following three introductory topics of data mining:

- Explaining cluster analysis
- Partitioning using k-means clustering
- Clustering using hierarchical techniques

As in the previous chapters, you learned through use cases. There are two different use cases provided that teach data mining with two different cluster analysis approaches. Before we begin working, it is worthwhile to understand cluster analysis in context.

Explaining clustering analysis

According to *Han (2011), Clustering is the process of grouping a set of data objects into multiple groups or clusters so that objects within a cluster have high similarity, but are very dissimilar to objects in other clusters (p. 443).*

Imagine a dinner party has just started. You see a medium-sized rectangular room with a number of people in it. The room is filled with people who are socializing. You notice that people have formed small groups. What draws them together? It could be their existing friendship. Perhaps it is a future networking opportunity. Some groups may form for less obvious reasons. One thing you can say is that it would be unlikely to see everyone in the center of the room talking together as a single group of people. Keep this mental image in your mind because it represents an underlying aspect of cluster analysis.

Clusters are collections of points from a multidimensional set of data such that they minimize the distance between each cluster's central point and its members. In this chapter, we will be talking about error. As you learned in `Chapter 4`, *Linear Regression for Business*, minimizing error plays a key role in developing analytic models. You will recall that regression had a response variable, such as `revenue`. **Supervised learning** is for cases when you have a response variable. You will use data features to predict that response.

People at the dinner party also have features such as age, height, weight, and income. However, while looking at groupings, you are not trying to predict a response. Cluster analysis is an unsupervised learning method. **Unsupervised learning** handles cases where you do not have a response variable. It provides a way to look at the people in that room (the observations) and determine ways to explain how they group together based on their features. Clusters form based on the similarity of observations compared to one another-the mean (central point).

In our dinner party example, the mean would be a location within the cluster representing the average position of all the people in this particular cluster. The central point will shift toward concentrations of people within a cluster, but remains within that cluster. Both panels of the following diagram show the same guests. The panel on the right shows groups and the cluster's labels positioned at the mean of the cluster:

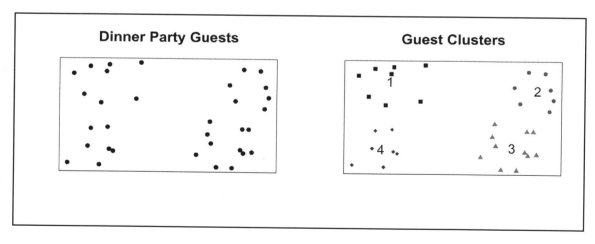

This chapter presents two types of cluster analysis methods: partitioning and clustering. Partitioning splits the entire set of data into a specified number of clusters based on similarities (proximity) of the points. Clustering differs from partitioning in that it splits or builds clusters by pairs based on similarity.

Partitioning using k-means clustering

The goal of partitioning is to place partitions and create clusters that reduce the within cluster sum of square error. In an extreme case, you could achieve a zero sum of square error if every data point existed in its own cluster. This would not be very useful though, would it? So partitioning is about finding the balance between reducing error and finding the right number of clusters.

A commonly used partitioning method is **k-means**. You will more often see it referred to as k-means clustering. K-means clustering places centers at k locations in the observation space to serve as the means of these k clusters. For example, if you were performing k-means clustering with $k = 3$, you would place three cluster means somewhere in the data space to set the initial conditions of the analysis.

K-means iteratively steps through the following three primary steps:

1. Specify the number of clusters, k. Assign their initial locations randomly or in specific locations.
2. The algorithm assigns all observations in the dataset to the nearest cluster.
3. The location of each cluster center is recalculated by calculating the mean of all members of the cluster across all dimensions.

Steps 2 and 3 repeat (reassigning points to clusters and then repositioning cluster centers) until there is no further movement of the clusters.

This brings up an important point. In partitioning techniques, you must specify the number of clusters for your analysis. What happens if you do not know how many clusters exist? We will discuss this in the following section, but there are business cases where the objectives inherently drive the number of clusters based on available resources or other realities of the market. Sometimes, you may have a sense of the number of clusters.

Use case: Customer Service Kiosk Placement

Bike Sharing LLC continues to grow each year. Management would like to increase the customer interaction by enhancing the business model. They have allocated a budget that supports the construction of up to three small customer service kiosks, strategically located in the Washington, D.C. metropolitan area.

The idea is to hire people to work in these kiosks throughout the day. The kiosks would provide a small number of products such as bands to protect riders' pants, city maps, water bottles, small snacks, and novelty items.

The representatives in the kiosks may also help casual users convert into registered users by answering questions and providing a more personalized experience.

Your job is to recommend the number and location of the kiosks. Your data is located in `Ch5_bike_station_locations.csv`, available at the `http://jgendron.github.io/com.packtpub.intro.r.bi/` website. The data contains the locations of the 244 Bike Sharing stations spread across the city. Location data are in latitude and longitude coordinates. Management has asked the business intelligence team to present its results as a business case-not only where to place the kiosks, but with an understanding of why. Their underlying goal is to place the customer service kiosks in areas of the city that have denser concentrations of bike stations. They would also like to minimize the total distance between bike stations and the nearest kiosk.

As you can see, you must find a proper balance in this problem. From the distance perspective, more kiosks would make them more accessible to riders. It would also increase the cost of construction, maintenance, and labor. However, having too few would make them farther from bike stations and could reduce the effect this management initiative aims to have. As you start studying this use case, consider these limitations, as well as ideas of future expansion if this initiative works out.

Exploring the data

Load the data into a `stations` data frame and then take a quick look at it:

```
stations <- read.csv("./data/Ch5_bike_station_locations.csv")
summary(stations)
```

We will get the following output:

```
      latitude              longitude
 Min.    :38.83       Min.    :-77.11
 1st Qu.:38.89       1st Qu.:-77.03
 Median :38.92       Median :-77.01
 Mean    :38.91       Mean    :-77.01
 3rd Qu.:38.94       3rd Qu.:-76.99
 Max.    :38.99       Max.    :-76.92
```

As you expected, the data is clean. There are no missing values and there is nothing particularly sophisticated about this data as it is just a list of bike stations and their geolocations. You will learn geo-mapping in `Chapter 7`, *Visualizing the Data's Story*, but you can still conduct some geo-based analysis using the `plot()` function due to the two-dimensional nature of the data itself:

```
hist(stations$latitude, col = 'gray')
hist(stations$longitude, ylim = c(0, 60), col = 'gray')
plot(stations$longitude, stations$latitude, asp = 1)
```

You will notice an `asp = 1` parameter in the `plot()` function. This maintains an aspect ratio of 1:1 on the *Y* and *X* axes. This keeps the plot from flattening and gives you a proper look at the geospatial data without using packages that are more sophisticated:

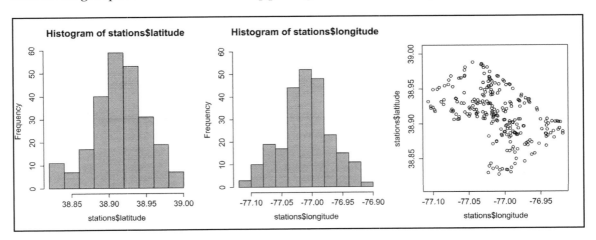

Even without using a more capable geo-mapping package, you can see the general outline of Washington, D.C. in the rightmost panel. It appears that Bike Sharing LLC has good bike station coverage throughout the city. Your visual inspection shows no clear pattern or groupings. It would be difficult to place two or three kiosks using visual inspection alone, so this is a good use of the k-means algorithm.

 The world is flat? All the examples in this chapter are two-dimensional in order to provide visualizations of what is going on. Once you enter higher dimensions, more advanced techniques are required to visualize the results. Sometimes you will rely only on a numeric output and measures to evaluate the clustering model as it is difficult to visualize high-dimensional data.

Running the kmeans() function

In Chapter 4, *Linear Regression for Business*, you saw how easy it is to invoke analytic functions such as lm() for linear regression. Using the kmeans() function is straightforward as well. Recall that the k-means algorithm can randomly place initial centers in the data space for you. Using the set.seed() function with the same number each time allows you to get repeatable results from random number generation. If you would like to follow along with the results shown in this section, set seed to a value of 123:

```
set.seed(123)
```

Now, you will create two R objects to hold the results of two k-means models, one with two clusters and another with three clusters. The constraints of the business problem drive the analysis to look at the options of two or three customer service kiosks:

```
two <- kmeans(stations, 2)
three <- kmeans(stations, 3)
```

This is all there is to building models. Now, you will interpret the output.

Interpreting the model output

You just created two models. You can inspect the output by typing the name of the object where you assigned the model. Look at the three-cluster k-means model by typing `three`:

```
K-means clustering with 3 clusters of sizes 57, 93, 94

Cluster means:
    latitude longitude
1 38.93327 -77.06502
2 38.87904 -76.97566
3 38.93765 -77.01089

Clustering vector:
  [1] 3 3 1 2 1 1 2 2 2 2 1 2 2 2 3 1 1 3 1 2 2 3 3 2 1 3 1 3 3 2 2 2 3 1 3 1 3 2
 [39] 3 3 2 3 1 3 2 3 2 1 2 1 2 3 2 2 2 2 2 3 2 1 1 1 3 2 2 2 3 3 3 3 3 3 3 2 3
 [77] 3 3 2 1 2 1 1 1 3 1 2 3 2 2 3 2 1 2 2 3 1 2 3 1 3 2 1 1 3 3 1 3 3 3 3 3 2 3
[115] 1 2 3 3 2 3 2 3 1 1 1 2 2 2 2 2 3 3 1 1 3 2 2 2 1 3 3 3 3 1 3 1 1 3 3 2 1 3
[153] 2 3 3 2 1 2 3 3 2 2 2 3 2 1 1 3 2 3 3 3 2 1 3 2 3 3 1 2 2 2 1 2 2 2 1 2 3
[191] 2 2 1 3 2 2 2 3 3 3 1 3 1 1 3 2 3 1 3 3 3 2 2 3 3 2 1 3 2 3 3 3 1 3 2 1 2 2 3
[229] 2 2 3 3 3 1 2 2 2 1 2 1 2 3 2 3

within cluster sum of squares by cluster:
[1] 0.04715762 0.12261951 0.07588127
 (between_SS / total_SS =  65.7 %)

Available components:

[1] "cluster"      "centers"      "totss"      "withinss"      "tot.withinss"
[6] "betweenss"    "size"         "iter"       "ifault"
```

The model output contains a great deal of information:

- This is a three-cluster model. The size of each cluster is **57**, **93**, and **94**.
- **Cluster means** provides the location of the center of each cluster.
- **Clustering vector** shows the cluster to which each data point is assigned.
- **Within cluster sum of squares by cluster** provides the sum of square error within each cluster, as well as a percentage showing how well the model accounted for error in the model. This model explains **65.7%** of the error.
- **Available components** shows all the items you can access for computation.

You can look at individual model elements using the `$` operator, similar to calling a data frame variable. Compare two-cluster `centers` and `size` with the three-cluster model. The input for two-cluster `centers` is as follows:

```
two$centers
```

The following is the output:

```
   latitude longitude
1  38.93855 -77.03975
2  38.88838 -76.97846
```

The input for two-cluster `size` is as follows:

```
two$size
```

The following is the output:

```
[1] 126 118
```

Learning to work with individual elements of the model is powerful. It allows you to create other data frames to isolate the data that is useful in solving your business problems. For instance, you know both models assigned each bike station to a cluster. In order to use this information in your analysis, you will create a data frame to capture the `$cluster` assignment of each observation and assign this to a variable.

Now, create a new `clus` data frame. Use the `cbind()` column-binding function to combine the existing `stations` data frame along with two new variables, `clus2` and `clus3`. You will place the cluster number for each observation by accessing `two$cluster` and `three$cluster`, and assigning this information to these variables respectively:

```
clus <- cbind(stations, clus2 = two$cluster,
              clus3 = three$cluster)
head(clus)
```

The output is shown here:

```
   latitude longitude clus2 clus3
1  38.95659 -76.99344     1     3
2  38.90522 -77.00150     2     3
3  38.98086 -77.05472     1     1
4  38.90293 -76.92991     2     2
5  38.94950 -77.09362     1     1
6  38.92780 -77.08474     1     1
```

The `head()` function shows you the first six observations of a data frame. Notice that the first two observations ended up in different clusters when applying the two-cluster and three-cluster models. Other observations, such as observations three through six, stayed in the same cluster in both models.

Developing a business case

You ran models for two and three clusters. You also learned how to extract information from the models. Now you will use these skills to develop a business case for the number of customer service kiosks and their locations. Begin by visualizing both models:

```
plot(clus$longitude, clus$latitude, col = two$cluster, asp = 1,
     pch = two$cluster, main = "Sites for two kiosks",
     xlab = "Longitude",  ylab = "Latitude")
points(two$centers[ ,2], two$centers[ ,1], pch = 23,
       col = 'maroon', bg = 'lightblue', cex = 3)
text(two$centers[ ,2], two$centers[ ,1], cex = 1.1,
     col = 'black', attributes(two$centers)$dimnames[[1]])

plot(clus$longitude, clus$latitude, col = three$cluster, asp = 1,
     pch = three$cluster, main = "Sites for three kiosks",
     xlab = "Longitude",  ylab = "Latitude")
points(three$centers[ ,2], three$centers[ ,1],
       pch = 23, col = 'maroon', bg = 'lightblue', cex = 3)
text(three$centers[ ,2], three$centers[ ,1], cex = 1.1,
     col = 'black', attributes(three$centers)$dimnames[[1]])
```

The output is shown in the following diagram:

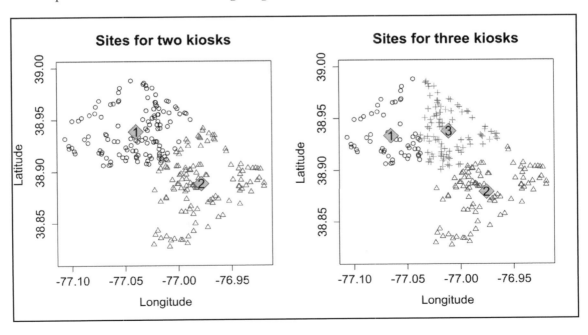

The plots show all the station locations, a colored shape indicating its cluster membership, and numbered diamonds representing the center of the cluster. If you were to compare the location of the cluster centers for both models, you would find the following information:

- Cluster 1 moves 2.26 kilometer (1.4 mile) to the west
- Cluster 2 moves 1.07 kilometer (0.7 mile) to the south

You will need to quantify the difference between these two models. Remember that marketing wants to know how a kiosk's location affects the distance from each station to the nearest kiosk. Therefore, the preceding information is not enough to answer the question.

R tip: The complete code for creating the plots is provided, so you can see the use of different par settings, as well as extracting information from the models. It also includes the use of `points()` to add the centers and `text()` to add text. Refer to R help to learn more details about using them. Intermediate-level plotting requires practice. Find opportunities to add new elements to your plots.

Fortunately, we can use visualization to look at the difference. Here are the basic steps and a code snippet used to generate a new `hybrid` data frame, creating the shapes to highlight cluster assignment differences to support the business case analysis:

1. Create a new `hybrid_shape` variable and fill it with zeros.
2. Loop through each of the observations.
3. Compare the cluster number that is assigned under both models.
4. Assign the hybrid shape based on the comparison results.

Visualizing differing cluster model effects

The following code will create different shapes to compare cluster assignment:

```
hybrid <- cbind(clus, hybrid_shape = rep(0,
dim(clus)[1]))
for (e in 1:dim(hybrid[1])[1]) {
    if (hybrid[e, 3] == hybrid[e, 4]) {
        hybrid[e, 5] <- hybrid[e, 3]
    }
    if (hybrid[e, 3] != hybrid[e, 4]) {
        hybrid[e, 5] <- hybrid[e ,3] + 15
    }
}
```

Now you can plot the results of this algorithmic approach:

```
plot(hybrid$longitude, hybrid$latitude, col = two$cluster,
    main = "Hybrid: Sites for two kiosks in three cluster
    locations", pch = hybrid$hybrid_shape, cex = 1.1,
    xlab = "Longitude",  ylab = "Latitude", asp = 1)
points(three$centers[1:2, 2], three$centers[1:2, 1],
        pch = 23, col = 'maroon', bg = 'lightblue', cex = 3)
text(three$centers[1:2, 2], three$centers[1:2, 1], cex = 1.1,
    col = 'black', attributes(two$centers)$dimnames[[1]])
```

We will get the following output:

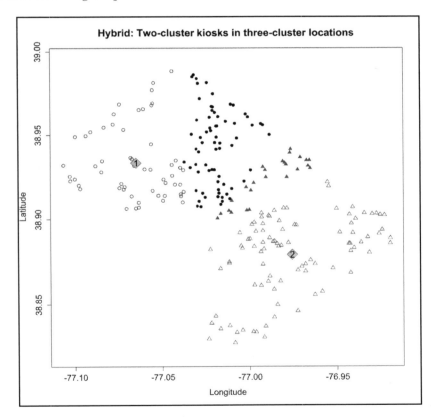

Based on the visualization, you believe that a good recommendation would be to build two customer service kiosks now, but they should be built in the locations as if there were three kiosks. This allows for future growth. If you make this recommendation, you anticipate the question: *how much will using a three-kiosk build plan impact the riders?*

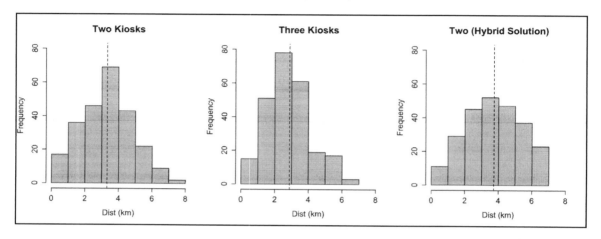

The previous panel plot shows the distribution of distances between each station and the nearest kiosk under all three situations. Here is a table comparing the alternatives:

measure	2-cluster	3-cluster	hybrid
mean distance	3.32 km	2.87 km	3.73 km
maximum distance	7.61 km	6.88 km	6.96 km

A distribution of distance increase using the hybrid approach is shown in the following diagram:

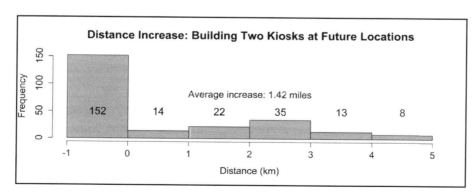

The calculations and plots show that the hybrid approach is a nice balance and gives some improvements over the two-cluster solution with growth options for the future.

 Learn more: Details of the distance calculations involve functions and other R techniques at intermediate level. You do not need to use R to support the business case calculations. For instance, a spreadsheet program would provide the same numbers. The complete R code base on the book's website at `http://jgendron.github.io/com.packtpub.intro.r.bi/` provides the calculations and functions that you can run to generate the same results as this business case analysis. The code is available in `Appendix D`, *R Code for Supporting Market Segment Business Case Calculations* as well.

Clustering using hierarchical techniques

Hierarchical clustering techniques approach the analysis a bit differently than k-means clustering. Instead of working with a predetermined number of centers and iterating to find membership, hierarchical techniques continually pair or split data into clusters based on similarity (distance). There are two different approaches:

- **Divisive clustering**: This begins with all the data in a single cluster and then splits it and all subsequent clusters until each data point is its own individual cluster
- **Agglomerative clustering**: This begins with each individual data point and pairs them together in a hierarchy until there is just one cluster

In this section, you will learn and use agglomerative hierarchical clustering. It is a bit faster than divisive clustering, but they both may work slow with very large datasets. One benefit of hierarchical approaches is that they do not require you to specify the number of clusters in advance. You can run the model and prune the hierarchical tree at the number of clusters you choose after seeing the entire model. There are evaluation techniques to help you choose the number of clusters in your final model. You will learn the evaluation techniques in this section.

Use case: Targeted Marketing Segments

Nice job on the kiosk project. Word gets around and the marketing group wants you to help them define customer segments and target advertising campaigns. Bike Sharing ridership has increased over 65% from 1,221,270 uses in 2011 to 2,028,912 uses in 2012, representing over 3.2 million bike shares.

You have been given the age and income data for over 8,000 existing customers. This `Ch5_age_income_data.csv` data is available on the book's website at

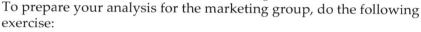

`http://jgendron.github.io/com.packtpub.intro.r.bi/`.

Your job is to use your skills to inspect and explore the data. Then, you will create various hierarchical clustering models and evaluate them to determine the number and characteristics of the customer segments. As you work through the problem, observe the number of analytic decisions you make-all affecting the final product. This will require you to use your analytic skills and business sense, blending science and art.

To prepare your analysis for the marketing group, do the following exercise:

1. Create a visualization of the data plotted as income versus age and color-code the points based on cluster membership
2. Provide tables indicating the relative size of each cluster, as well as the minimum, median, and maximum age and income within each cluster

You have done a great job since you have been working with R and the team, and you will do great with this analysis as well. Have fun and appreciate the subtle aspects of model selection. It will serve you well in the future.

Cleaning and exploring data

You are familiar with this phase by now. Cleaning and exploring data is something you typically do before each analysis. To review it, refer to the following steps:

- **Cleaning: summarize-fix-convert-adapt (SFCA)**
- **Exploring: look-relationships-correlation-significance (LRCS)**

Load the data into a `market` data frame:

```
market <- read.csv("./data/Ch5_age_income_data.csv")
str(market)
```

The output is as follows:

```
'data.frame': 8105 obs. of  3 variables:
 $ bin   : Factor w/ 8 levels "10-19","20-29",..: 6 3 2 3 7 6 8 5 ...
 $ age   : int  64 33 24 33 78 62 88 54 54 31 ...
 $ income: num  87083 76808 12044 61972 60120 ...
```

 Real World? This use case only involves two variables and is not typical in the business world. This approach is simplistic, but it teaches the skills while allowing for visualization that is not possible with higher dimension problems.

Let's see the following code:

```
summary(market)
```

It will return the following output:

```
      bin             age             income
 20-29  :2091   Min.   :18.00   Min.   :    233.6
 30-39  :1883   1st Qu.:28.00   1st Qu.: 43792.7
 40-49  :1267   Median :39.00   Median : 65060.0
 50-59  :1118   Mean   :42.85   Mean   : 66223.6
 60-69  : 798   3rd Qu.:55.00   3rd Qu.: 85944.7
 70-79  : 478   Max.   :89.00   Max.   :178676.4
 (Other): 470
```

`summary` tells you that the data is clean and contains no `NA` values requiring fixes. What about data type conversions? They all look appropriate for your analysis. Is there anything else? You have already looked at the variables in the summary. Now see if there are any relationships among the variables:

```
boxplot(market$age ~ market$bin, main = "Explore Age")
boxplot(market$income ~ market$bin, main = "Explore Income")
```

The output is as shown here:

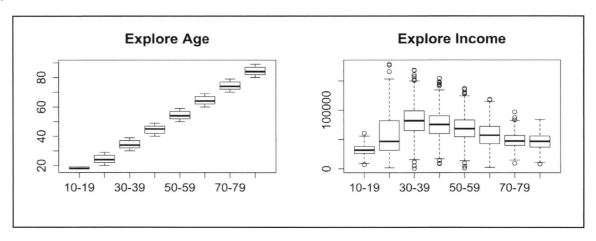

The left panel shows no improperly binned ages. The right panel shows a relationship between age and income, and this is not surprising. Is there a correlation?

Running the `cor.test(market$age, market$income)` code provides a correlation of `-0.05994158` and a p-value of `6.648e-08`. This shows a mild negative correlation and the p-value indicates that despite the mild correlation, it is also significant. You can see in the previous figure that the relationship shows piecewise correlation-positively below 40 years of age and negatively above it. The relationship is nonlinear.

Try this: Split the market data into two subsets, using 40 as the breakpoint, and check the correlation of income versus people less than 40 and for people 40 and older. Try it and see if you can get these piecewise correlation values:

- Age < 40: `correlation = 0.5624`
- Age >= 40: `correlation = -0.4674`

Hint: Use the `filter()` function from the `dplyr` library to assign the result of this operation (`filter(market, age < 40)`) to a new data frame. Then, do the same for `>= 40`. Run the `cor()` function on both data frames.

Good. There is only one thing left for you to check. Do you need to adapt any data to suit your analytic needs? This is a tough question. Consider the units (scale) of the two variables. We have age in tens and income in tens of thousands. Clustering techniques work on distance measures, so what happens with the income variables that are 1,000 times larger than age? A demonstration using a k-means plot shows the effect:

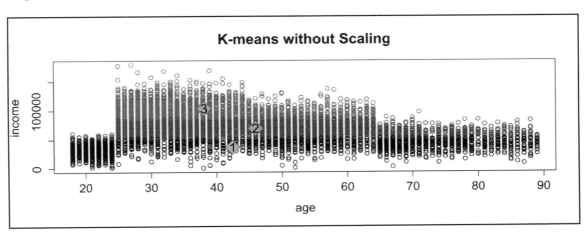

Hmmm…that is not what we expected. Why? Clustering relies on a measure of distance, and in this case, the scale of the age variable is smaller, relative to income, so it dominates the clustering. Each cluster grabbed all the data across the entire range of age because they are all closer to one another (in value) than to any income data points. You will need to normalize the data by scaling and centering it. R has a function called scale(). This function centers the data by subtracting the variable's mean from each observation. Likewise, it scales the data by dividing each observation by a scaling factor.

R tip: You can specify the scaling. This may be a custom scaling factor, the standard deviation of the variable, or its root mean square. The default is to use standard deviation. Type ?scale in your console to get a complete explanation.

You can add the centered and scaled transformation as new columns (variables) to the data frame. The scale() function outputs a matrix, so you need to convert it using the as.numeric() function into a data type that can be added to the market data frame:

```
market$age_scale <- as.numeric(scale(market$age))
market$inc_scale <- as.numeric(scale(market$income))
```

The following is the same k-means plot after scaling. Notice the difference:

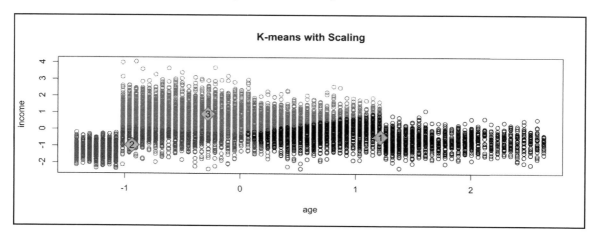

Good job. You cleaned and explored the data and are ready for analysis. Remember from Chapter 2, *Data Cleaning* that you can expect to spend 80% of your time in this crucial phase. Now, it is time to learn how to perform hierarchical clustering.

Running the hclust() function

This step is remarkably easy, much like using the k-means model. One call to the `hclust()` function will take the data, run a hierarchical clustering model, and output the model into an object. The real skill is in knowing how to interpret the results:

```
set.seed(456)
hc_mod <- hclust(dist(market[ ,4:5]), method = "ward.D2")
```

The following is a summary explanation of this function call:

- `hc_mod` is the variable used to hold the hierarchical clustering model.
- `dist()` is required because `hclust()` works using a distance matrix. A distance matrix is a square matrix that compares every data point with its distance from every other data point. In our case, this matrix will be 8105 x 8105, with zeros down the diagonal.
- `[ ,4:5]` is a subset of the market data frame. Specifically, the two columns containing the normalized (centered and scaled) ages and incomes.

- `ward.D2` is the clustering algorithm used. There are a few algorithms to choose from. Ward D is often used due to its speed and practicality. It is the same as using the **agglomerative nesting (AGNES)** method. **Divisive analysis (DIANA)** is used for divisive clustering.

 Learn more: Check out the R help on `?dist` and `?hclust`. These explain more about the various distance methods and the different types of clustering methods available. Learn more about other clustering approaches at `http://www.stat.berkeley.edu/~s133/Cluster2a.html`.

Visualizing the model output

Running a hierarchical clustering generates an object. In order to interpret the object, you will need to convert it into a dendrogram. A **dendrogram** is a tree-like hierarchical structure that organizes the results of the clustering for interpretation. The `as.dendrogram()` function converts the `hclust` object into a dendrogram. You can then visualize it using the `plot()` function:

```
dend <- as.dendrogram(hc_mod)
library(dendextend)
dend_six_color <- color_branches(dend, k = 6)
plot(dend_six_color, leaflab = "none", horiz = TRUE,
     main = "Age and Income Dendrogram", xlab = "Height")
abline(v = 37.5, lty = 'dashed', col = 'blue')
```

Here is an explanation of the preceding parameters shown in bold:

- Adding color can help the clusters stand out. The `dendextend` library provides the ability to add color, as well as other functionality.
- The `color_branches()` function takes the dendrogram and the number of clusters as parameters. You can set $k = 6$ to specify six clusters.

- Two other parameters help customize your plot: `leaflab = "none"` will suppress the 8,105 numerical labels at the end of the dendrogram and `horiz = TRUE` will plot the dendrogram with the heights along the x-axis.

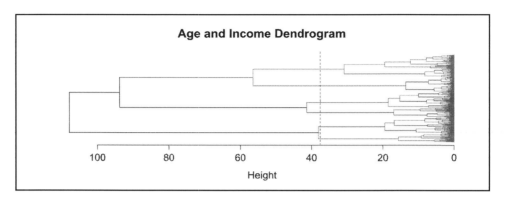

Height is an indication of the strength of the separation among branches. Greater differences in branch heights indicate stronger clustering. It looks like the height, 37.5, is a good cut point for six clusters. You can see that the dashed line at 37.5 cuts through six branches, hence six clusters. For readers viewing this in print form, the color version of this plot is available to you in the book repository. You can find this particular plot at `https://github.com/jgendron/com.packtpub.intro.r.bi/blob/master/Chapter5-Cluste ringAnalysis/graphics/color_dendrogram.png`.

Lastly, running `str()` for any height provides additional information on the dendrogram:

```
str(cut(dend, h = 37.5)$upper)
```

It will return the following output:

```
--[dendrogram w/ 2 branches and 6 members at h = 108]
  |--[dendrogram w/ 2 branches and 2 members at h = 38]
  |   |--leaf "Branch 1" (h= 15.7 midpoint = 274, x.member = 782 )
  |   `--leaf "Branch 2" (h= 19.5 midpoint = 628, x.member = 1526 )
  `--[dendrogram w/ 2 branches and 4 members at h = 93.8]
      |--[dendrogram w/ 2 branches and 2 members at h = 41.3]
      |   |--leaf "Branch 3" (h= 17 midpoint = 431, x.member = 905 )
      |   `--leaf "Branch 4" (h= 18.5 midpoint = 463, x.member = 1473 )
      `--[dendrogram w/ 2 branches and 2 members at h = 56.4]
          |--leaf "Branch 5" (h= 13.6 midpoint = 530, x.member = 1323 )
          `--leaf "Branch 6" (h= 30.8 midpoint = 753, x.member = 2096
```

Sometimes hierarchical clustering helps determine the number of clusters. You are going to build nine different k-means models and compare how well they explain the variance among group membership. We are doing this for the following two reasons:

- To show you a way to evaluate the increased accuracy (reduction in error) by increasing clusters in order to find an appropriate number of clusters
- To compare the clustering patterns that emerge from the two methods and give you options for developing your business case to the marketing team

Running multiple k-means models is as simple as creating a variable to hold each model object. Set a randomization seed and then build nine models containing from 2 through 10 clusters using the scaled variables in the `market` dataset (columns four and five).

Try this: If you are comfortable with the language you just read, then congratulations. You are starting to get a practical feel for clustering techniques.

Go ahead and create nine k-means models on the scaled data in the `market` data frame. For example, five clusters is `five <- kmeans(market[,4:5], 5)`. Use `set.seed(456)` for repeatability. The complete code for building the k-means models is in the code base. Other aspects of k-means, such as plotting, do not appear in this section due to space, but the code is available in the code base as well.

Evaluating the models

When you have the option of choosing the number of clusters, you can evaluate the benefit versus complexity of adding more clusters using a measure from the k-means model and something called **the elbow method** (*Han, 2011*). The elbow method plots the within cluster sum of square error versus the number of clusters. You can then find the elbow in the curve, where increasing clusters does not improve the sum of square error:

1. Create an `optimize` data frame to generate a plot for the elbow method.
2. Fill the `clusters` variable with the numbers 2 through 10 using `c(2:10)`.
3. Initialize the `wss` variable with zeros to hold `$tot.withinss` for each model.
4. Fill the `wss` variable with the result of `as.numeric(model$tot.withinss)`.

Let's look at the code:

```
optimize <- data.frame(clusters = c(2:10), wss = rep(0, 9))
optimize[1, 2] <- as.numeric(two$tot.withinss)
optimize[2, 2] <- as.numeric(three$tot.withinss)
optimize[3, 2] <- as.numeric(four$tot.withinss)
optimize[4, 2] <- as.numeric(five$tot.withinss)
optimize[5, 2] <- as.numeric(six$tot.withinss)
optimize[6, 2] <- as.numeric(seven$tot.withinss)
optimize[7, 2] <- as.numeric(eight$tot.withinss)
optimize[8, 2] <- as.numeric(nine$tot.withinss)
optimize[9, 2] <- as.numeric(ten$tot.withinss)
plot(optimize$wss ~ optimize$clusters, type = "b",
    ylim = c(0, 12000), ylab = 'Within Sum of Square Error',
    main = 'Finding Optimal Number of Clusters Based on Error',
    xlab = 'Number of Clusters', pch = 17, col = 'black')
```

We will get the following output:

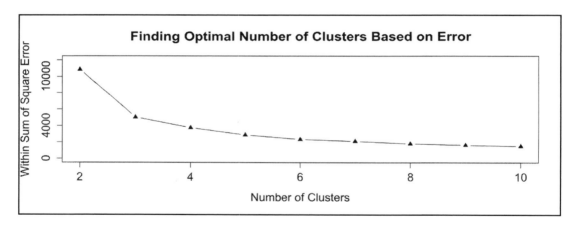

Based on the elbow method, there is little apparent benefit from having more than six clusters. A reasonable question is whether that is too many marketing campaigns to manage. There were over three million individual rentals over the two-year period. That is a large enough population to explore as many as six clusters for marketing. How did k-means breakdown these clusters? You can use the $size attribute to see:

```
three$size; four$size; five$size; six$size; seven$size
```

The output is as follows:

```
[1] 2460 2141 3504
[1] 2380 1440 2271 2014
[1] 1325 1788 1882 1612 1498
[1] 1110 1758 1308 1180 1511 1238
[1] 1092 1454  937 1023 1133  783 1683
```

It looks like five or six clusters give reasonable target markets and reduced error. We can compare them by getting a sense of the demographics in five-cluster versus six-cluster modeling:

1. Add a clus5 variable to the market data frame and add cluster assignments.
2. Create a five-cluster pruned dendrogram using cutree and k = 5.
3. Add a dend5 variable and five-cluster assignments from the dendrogram.
4. Repeat steps **1 – 3** for a six-cluster k-means and dendrogram using k = 6.

This is shown in the following code snippet:

```
market$clus5 <- five$cluster
dend_five <- cutree(dend, k = 5)
market$dend5 <- dend_five

market$clus6 <- six$cluster
dend_six <- cutree(dend, k = 6)
market$dend6 <- dend_six
```

You have added four columns to the market data frame to signify the cluster each observation was assigned to, under all four models.

Choosing a model

You can use visualization to help in model selection. Plot the two-dimensional clustering patterns for both methods over five and six clusters:

```
par(mfrow = c(2, 2), mar = c(3, 4, 4, 2) + 0.1)
plot(market$age, market$income, col = five$cluster,
     pch = five$cluster, xlab = '', main = '5-means Clustering')
plot(market$age, market$income, col = six$cluster, xlab = '',
     ylab = '', pch = six$cluster, main = '6-means Clustering')
par(mar = c(5, 4, 2, 2) + 0.1)
plot(market$age, market$income, col = market$dend5,
     pch = market$dend5, main = 'k = 5 Hierarchical')
plot(market$age, market$income, col = market$dend6, ylab = '',
```

```
        pch = market$dend6, main = 'k = 6 Hierarchical')
par(mfrow = c(1, 1), mar = c(5, 4, 4, 2) + 0.1)
```

This is where the power of visualization and the art of business will influence the numerical aspects of what you have been doing. This phase can take some time in real-world cases. It is a thoughtful process. Let's point out two characteristics of the different modeling approaches as shown in the following figure:

- K-means edges are not as jagged. It works based on distance from a center.
- Agglomerative hierarchical clustering groups by similarity, but you can find patterns that are not as spherical.

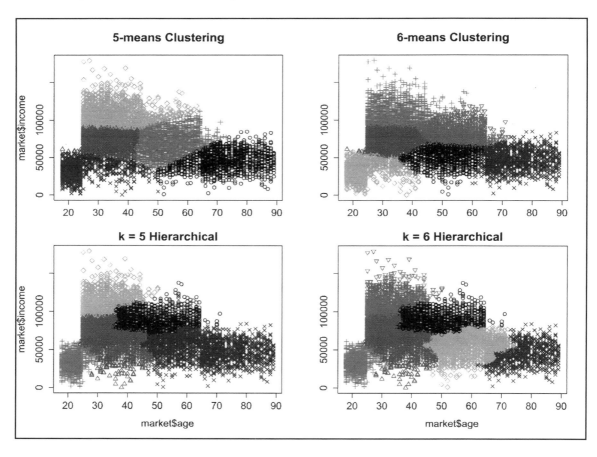

For example, hierarchical clustering gives a more ragged edge, such as the *noses* in the hierarchical plots at *age = 45* and *income = 60,000*. This also makes a difference in how the region between 30-50 years of age from 0-50,000 income appears. You will also see more income banding in k-means plots versus hierarchical plots. This raises the practical question: which of these represents a business understanding of the market more closely? The following are some observations and considerations that you will notice:

- In bike riding, age is an important factor for marketing
- The hierarchical models separate the lower income band into more age bins:
  - Younger users, as well as middle aged in the 30's through 50's
  - Older users display some type of division around retirement age
  - A *stovepipe* in the 30-35 range with only two bands of income
  - The 35-60 range adds a specific cluster from $70-140 thousand

BI tip: Visualizing information is essential in business intelligence. Whether it is for the purpose of creating a dashboard or presentation, a good visual can make all the difference. Sharpen your plotting skills in R. Type `?par` to keep learning more.

These observations make some practical marketing sense. Regarding the 30-something aged customers, perhaps there is some wisdom in thinking of them more in terms of age and less in terms of income. On the other hand, the k-means approach has a large cluster in the lower left, hierarchical modeling creates a smaller demographic representing the youngest and lowest income. This could be the decisive tone of a successful marketing campaign.

You can certainly develop alternative conclusions, but after some time looking at these, we will decide to focus on the results from the six-cluster hierarchical model. Now, you will prepare the material for your final recommendation to the marketing group.

Preparing the results

You are all set. Now let's recall what the marketing group requested from the BI team.

To prepare your analysis for the marketing group, perform the following exercise:

1. Create a visualization of the data plotted as income versus age and color-code the points based on cluster membership.
2. Provide tables indicating the relative size of each cluster, as well as the minimum, median, and maximum age and income within each cluster.

For visualization, you will need to generate the cluster centers manually as the `hclust` object does not have an element such as `$centers` from a `kmeans` object. You can do this by using the `dplyr` package you know and creating a `labels` data frame with the medians for `age` and `income` grouped by cluster assignment (found in the `dend6` variable):

```
library(dplyr)
labels <- as.data.frame(market %>%
    group_by(dend6) %>%
    summarise(avg_age = median(age), avg_inc = median(income)))
```

The resulting data frame will have six rows and three columns: a column with each of the six cluster numbers, a column with the median age of all assigned to each cluster, and a column with the median income for all assigned to each cluster. This is similar to the output that a k-means model produces, and we will use this data to plot our cluster labels:

```
plot(market$age, market$income, col = market$dend6,
    pch = market$dend6 - 1, xlab = "Age", ylab = "Income",
    main = 'Marketing Clusters from Hierarchical Clustering \n (Labels
show medians of age and income for cluster)')
points(labels[ ,2], labels[ ,3], pch = 21, col = 'maroon',
    bg = 'white', cex = 3)
text(labels[ ,2], labels[ ,3], cex = 1.1, col = 'black',
    labels[ ,1])
```

The output creates the visualization asked for by marketing in the following diagram:

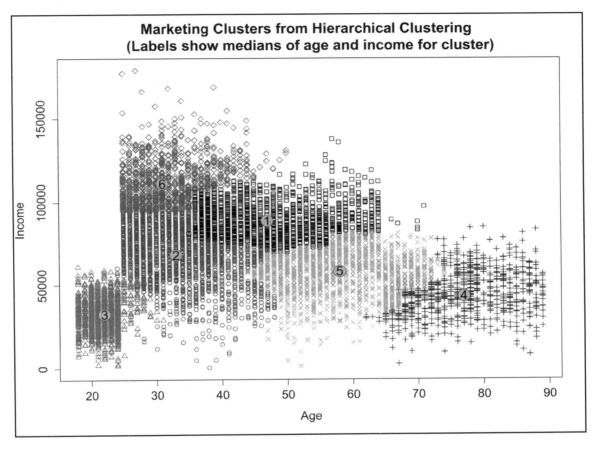

Now you need two tables indicating the relative size of each cluster, as well as the minimum, median, and maximum age and income within each cluster. Using `dplyr` once again, you can pipe (`%>%`) the `market` data frame to the `group_by` cluster and get your summary statistics. Use `n()` for your count, and `min`, `median`, and `max` as you would expect:

```
market %>% group_by(dend6) %>% summarise(ClusterSize = n())
```

We will get the following output:

	dend6 (int)	ClusterSize (int)
1	1	1473
2	2	2096

3	3	1323
4	4	782
5	5	1526
6	6	905

Let's see the following code snippet:

```
market %>% group_by(dend6) %>%
    summarise(min_age = min(age), med_age = median(age),
              max_age = max(age), med_inc = median(income),
              min_inc = min(income), max_inc = max(income))
```

This returns the table requested by marketing as shown in the following output:

dend6 (int)	min_age (int)	med_age (dbl)	max_age (int)	med_inc (dbl)	min_inc (dbl)	max_inc (dbl)
1	1	35	47	71	88170.32	69491.7763	137557.18
2	2	24	33	48	67957.66	233.6338	94708.92
3	3	18	22	31	32329.49	1484.8486	60887.37
4	4	62	77	89	43044.21	2319.2740	84300.56
5	5	44	58	74	57806.34	973.4146	81988.14
6	6	25	31	50	111124.93	93826.6611	178676.37

Summary

In this chapter, you learned a lot about the unsupervised learning technique called cluster analysis. It helps you when you do not have a response variable but you believe that there are natural groupings in the data. There are many types of clustering algorithms, and you learned two. K-means clustering is widely used and is ideal when you have constraints or a sense of how many clusters exist in your data. It is straightforward to implement and you can pull elements out of the model to perform other analysis. You used k-means to determine the best number and location of customer service kiosks. Hierarchical clustering is a good choice when you do not have a sense of the number of groups that may exist in the data. You used this to perform customer segmentation of two-dimensional demographic data. You learned how to use the elements from k-means to help evaluate the right number of clusters to select, as well as visualize the output of hierarchical clustering.

In the next chapter, you will learn the last analytic technique presented in this book. Time series analysis is a way to work with data when there are dependencies among the observations, especially when it is time-based. You will also learn about trends and seasonality.

6
Time Series Analysis

Time series analysis is the most difficult analysis technique presented in this book. One may argue that it does not belong in an introductory book. It is true that this is a challenging topic. However, one may also argue that an introductory awareness of a difficult topic is better than perfect ignorance of it. **Time series analysis** is a technique designed to look at chronologically ordered data that may form cycles over time. Key topics covered in this chapter include the following:

- Analyzing time series data with linear regression
- Introducing key elements of time series analysis
- Building ARIMA time series models

Time series analysis is an upper-level college statistics course. It is also a demanding topic taught in econometrics. This chapter provides you with an understanding of a useful but difficult analysis technique. It provides a combination of theoretical learning and hands-on practice. The goal is to provide you with a basic understanding of working with time series data and give you a foundation to learn more.

Use case: Forecasting Future Ridership
The finance group approached the BI team and asked for help with forecasting future trends. They heard about your great work for the marketing team and wanted to get your perspective on their problem.

Once a year they prepare an annual report that includes ridership details. They are hoping to include not only last year's ridership levels, but also a forecast of ridership levels in the coming year. These types of time-based predictions are **forecasts**. The Ch6_ridership_data_2011-2012.csv data file is available at the book's website at http://jgendron.github.io/com.packtpub.intro.r.bi/.

This data is a subset of the bike sharing data you used in the first two chapters. It contains two years of observations, including the date and a count of users by hour. Your task is to convert this data into a time series aggregated by month, apply a time series model, and produce a monthly forecast for the coming year.

Analyzing time series data with linear regression

You learned how to predict responses using linear regression in `Chapter 4`, *Linear Regression for Business*; however, this technique is less useful and sometimes not even appropriate to analyzing time series data. *Why?* This question is the catalyst to understand the proper application of time series models.

Before working with the data from the use case, we will use a dataset already in R. The `TSA` package contains a dataset called **airpass**. This dataset provides the total monthly count of international airline passengers covering the period from January 1960 to December 1971. This represents twelve years of monthly passenger data, which is 144 observations. After loading the library, the `airpass` dataset is available using the `data()` function. You can examine the dataset using methods discussed in the previous chapters:

```
library(TSA)
data(airpass)
str(airpass)
summary(airpass)
```

The output is as follows:

```
Time-Series [1:144] from 1960 to 1972: 112 118 132 129 121 135 ...
   Min. 1st Qu.  Median   Mean 3rd Qu.    Max.
  104.0   180.0   265.5  280.3   360.5   622.0
```

This is a time series. This means that responses are dependent on previous points in time. *This dependent data would fail the assumption of independence.* What would a linear regression look like anyway? The following is code to create a temporary data frame to generate a linear model. Begin by extracting passenger volume and assigning the single column as a matrix to the `volume` variable:

```
volume <- as.matrix(airpass)
```

That was easy. Now you need to create a time variable. A time series naturally contains time data, but it is not a variable. It is contained in the data type. You can extract it using the time() function. This provides a decimal value representing the month and year. For example, July, 1960 is the halfway point of that year so that time returns as 1960.500:

```
time <- as.matrix(time(airpass))
```

Good job…you are learning some extra R approaches to help you manipulate datasets. The last step is to create a data frame called airpass_df by combining the two vectors, volume and time, using the cbind() function. You need to name the columns in order to plot them. This is done with the colnames() function:

```
airpass_df <- as.data.frame(cbind(volume, time))
colnames(airpass_df) <- c("volume", "time")
```

Create a linear model, lmfit. Then, use summary(lmfit) to see the model results:

```
lmfit <- lm(volume ~ time, data = airpass_df)
summary(lmfit)
```

We will get the following output:

```
Call:
lm(formula = volume ~ time, data = airpass_df)

Residuals:
    Min      1Q  Median      3Q     Max
-93.858 -30.727  -5.757  24.489 164.999
Coefficients:
              Estimate Std. Error t value Pr(>|t|)
(Intercept) -62406.656   2178.265  -28.65   <2e-16 ***
time            31.886      1.108   28.78   <2e-16 ***
---
Signif. codes:  0 '***' 0.001 '**' 0.01 '*' 0.05 '.' 0.1 ' ' 1

Residual standard error: 46.06 on 142 degrees of freedom
Multiple R-squared:  0.8536,    Adjusted R-squared:  0.8526
F-statistic: 828.2 on 1 and 142 DF,  p-value: < 2.2e-16
```

Wait a minute. This shows an apparently good model. Recall the things that you need to check:

- F-statistic and p-value: These look good
- Significant coefficients: `time` is statistically significant
- Adjusted R-squared: The model explains over 85% of the error

The term **LINE** helps us remember the required assumptions of **linearity**, **independence**, **normality**, and **equal variance**. Recall that this dependent data would fail the assumption of independence, but we can check the other three assumptions of linear regression.

Linearity, normality, and equal variance

Refer to `Chapter 4`, *Linear Regression for Business*, if you want to review the code used to check the following three assumptions:

```
par(mfrow = c(1, 3))
plot(airpass_df$time, airpass_df$volume, pch = 19, main = "Linearity?")
abline(lmfit)
hist(lmfit$residuals, main = "Normality?", col = "gray")
plot(lmfit$fitted.values, lmfit$residuals, main = "Equal Variance?",
     pch = 19)
abline(h = 0)
```

The output is shown as follows:

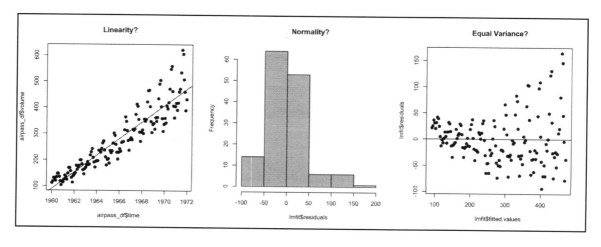

This plot shows data that is **generally linear**, although you do see a bit of an upward curvature in the leftmost panel. The data does not meet the assumption of **normality** based on the histogram of residuals. Lastly, the assumption of **equal variance** of the residuals fails as well. Notice the curved and fanned-shape plot in the rightmost panel.

Prediction and confidence intervals

Plotting the 95% confidence and prediction intervals along with the fitted line will help reveal why linear regression is inappropriate for this time-based data-as the assumption tests have already shown.

Here are the major code elements in the following block:

- `newdata` creates the input variables to predict responses
- `seq()` creates a sequence of numbers from `1960` to `1972` in steps of `2`
- `predict.lm()` uses `newdata` to make the predictions
- `points()` and `abline()` add the predicted points and interval lines

To plot the 95% confidence and prediction intervals, we will use the following code:

```
plot(airpass, main = "95 Percent Confidence and Prediction Intervals of
airpass Data")
abline(lmfit, col = "blue")
newdata <- data.frame(time = seq(1960, 1972, 2))
pred <- predict.lm(lmfit, newdata, interval = "predict")
points(seq(1960, 1972, 2), pred[ ,1], pch = 19, col = "blue")
abline(lsfit(seq(1960, 1972, 2), pred[ ,2]), col = "red")
abline(lsfit(seq(1960, 1972, 2), pred[ ,3]), col = "red")
pred <- predict.lm(lmfit, newdata, interval = "confidence")
abline(lsfit(seq(1960, 1972, 2), pred[,2]), lty = 2, col = "red")
abline(lsfit(seq(1960, 1972, 2), pred[,3]), lty = 2, col = "red")
```

The output is shown in the following diagram:

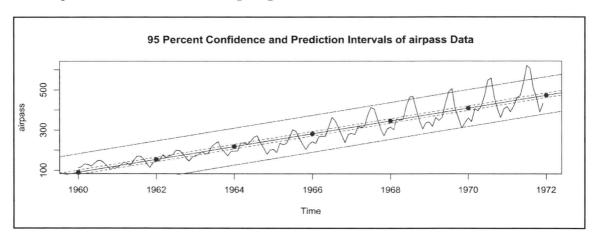

The linear model is a terrible predictor of these dependent, time-based values. All predictions will fall on the center line-the trend. It will not capture the predictable cycles that you see. In addition, some forecasts systemically appear outside the confidence interval, which indicates an underlying issue with the model. You will need to use another type of regression called time series analysis.

Forecasts versus predictions: In linear regression, you made **predictions**. You predicted a response using other variables-not previous responses. With time series analysis, you will make a forecast. The **forecast** is a number of future responses, based on the previous responses themselves. Consider the price of a house. Here is how you would make a prediction and forecast:

- **Prediction**: You can predict the sales price based on variables that influence the response, such as crime, access to transportation, and schools
- **Forecast**: You can forecast the sales price based on a time series model using the previous sales prices themselves to forecast future prices

Introducing key elements of time series analysis

You just applied a linear regression model to time series data and saw it did not work. The biggest problem was not a failure in fitting a linear model to the trend. For this well-behaved time series, the average formed a linear plot over time. *Where was the problem?*

The problem was in seasonal fluctuations. The seasonal fluctuations were one year in length and then repeated. Most of the data points existed above and below the fitted line, instead of on it or near it. As we saw, the ability to make a point estimate prediction was poor. There is an old adage that says *even a broken clock is correct twice a day*. This is a good analogy for analyzing seasonal time series data with linear regression. The fitted linear line will be a good predictor twice every cycle. You will need to do something about the seasonal fluctuations in order to make better forecasts; otherwise, they will simply be straight lines with no account of the seasonality.

With seasonality in mind, there are functions in R that can break apart the trend, seasonality, and random components of a time series. The decompose() function found in the forecast package shows how each of these three components influence the data. You can think of this technique as being similar to creating the correlogram plot during exploratory data analysis. It captures a greater understanding of the data in a single plot:

```
library(forecast)
plot(decompose(airpass))
```

The output of this code is shown here:

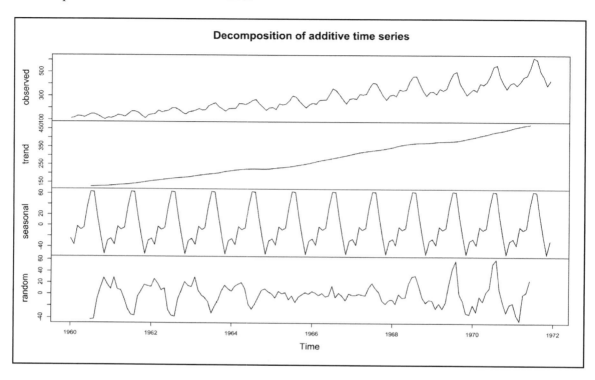

This decomposition capability is nice as it gives you insights about approaches you may want to take with the data. Referring to the previous figure, each plot is described as follows:

- The top panel provides a view of the original data for context.
- The next panel shows the trend. It smooths the data and removes the seasonal component. In this case, you will see that over time, air passenger volume has increased steadily and in the same direction.
- The third plot shows the seasonal component. Removing the trend helps reveal any seasonal cycles. This data shows a regular and repeated seasonal cycle through the years.
- The final plot is the randomness-everything else in the data. It is like the error term in linear regression. You will see fewer errors in the middle of the series.

The stationary assumption

There is an assumption for creating time series models. The data must be stationary. **Stationary** data exists when its mean and variance do not change as a function of time. If you decompose a time series and witness a trend, seasonal component, or both, then you have non-stationary data. You can transform them into stationary data in order to meet the required assumption.

Using a linear model for comparison, there is randomness around a mean-represented by data points scattered randomly around a fitted line. The data is independent of time and it does not follow other data in a cycle. This means that the data is stationary. Not all the data lies on the fitted line, but it is not *moving*. In order to analyze time series data, you need your data points to stay still.

Imagine trying to count a class of primary school students while they are on the playground during recess. They are running about back and forth. In order to count them, you need them to stay still-be stationary. Transforming non-stationary data into stationary data allows you to analyze it. You can transform non-stationary data into stationary data using a technique called differencing.

Differencing techniques

Differencing subtracts each data point from the data point that is immediately in front of it in the series. This is done with the `diff()` function. Mathematically, it works as follows:

$$y\_diff\_trend = y_{(t+1)} - y_t$$

Seasonal differencing is similar, but it subtracts each data point from its related data point in the next cycle. This is done with the `diff()` function, along with a `lag` parameter set to the number of data points in a cycle. Mathematically, it works as follows:

$$y\_diff\_seasonal = y_{(t+lag)} - y_t$$

Look at the results of differencing in this toy example. Build a small sample dataset of 36 data points that include an upward trend and seasonal component, as shown here:

```
seq_down <- seq(.625, .125, -0.125)
seq_up <- seq(0, 1.5, 0.25)
y <- c(seq_down, seq_up, seq_down + .75, seq_up + .75, seq_down + 1.5,
        seq_up + 1.5)
```

Then, plot the original data and the results obtained after calling the `diff()` function:

```
par(mfrow = c(1, 3))
plot(y, type = "b", ylim = c(-.1, 3))
plot(diff(y), ylim = c(-.1, 3), xlim = c(0, 36))
plot(diff(diff(y), lag = 12), ylim = c(-.1, 3), xlim = c(0, 36))
par(mfrow = c(1, 1))
detach(package:TSA, unload=TRUE)
```

Detach the `TSA` package to avoid conflicts with other functions in the `forecast` library we will use. The following three panels show the results of differencing and seasonal differencing:

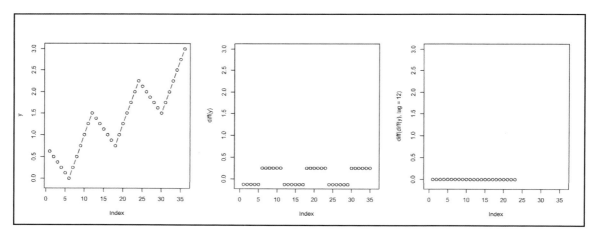

These three panels are described as follows:

- The left panel shows n = 36 data points, with 12 points in each of the three cycles. It also shows a steadily increasing trend. Either of these characteristics breaks the stationary data assumption.

- The center panel shows the results of differencing. Plotting the difference between each point and its next neighbor removes the trend. Also, notice that you get one less data point. With differencing, you get $(n - 1)$ results.
- The right panel shows seasonal differencing with a lag of 12. The data is stationary. Notice that the trend differencing is now the data in the seasonal differencing. Also note that you will lose a cycle of data, getting $(n - lag)$ results.

Building ARIMA time series models

The term ARIMA is made up of the letters that represent a modeling approach for time series data. ARIMA models contain the following three elements:

- **AR**: **Auto regressive**, specified with p or P
- **I**: **Integrated** (differencing), specified with d or D
- **MA**: **Moving average**, specified with q or Q

Auto regressive means that earlier lagged points in the data influence later points in the sequence. This creates a dependence condition. The type of AR model chosen is based on how many steps away (lags) the points in the past affect the points in the future. Data that has a greater lingering effect on future points has a higher lag. The higher the lag, the higher the AR number. You will see models referred to as *AR(1)*, *AR(2)*, and so forth to represent an autoregressive model of the number of p lags specified in the parentheses.

Integrated refers to differencing that you learned earlier. The d value represents the number of differences used in the model. It is typically zero or one.

Moving average is the technique of calculating a future point based on the residuals (the error) of previous terms. You will see models referred to as *MA(1)*, *MA(2)*, and so forth to represent a moving average model with the number of q lagged forecast errors specified in the parentheses.

Models are referred to as *ARIMA(p, d, q)(P, D, Q)*. The first group of numbers represents modeling of the non-seasonal components and the second group of numbers represents modeling of the seasonal components. The sequences can be different for each.

Selecting a model to make forecasts

Correlation plots help you determine the type of model and number of lags to use. There is an **autocorrelation function** (**ACF**) plot and a **partial autocorrelation function** (**PACF**) plot. These plots show the amount of correlation between various lags of a time series. You can use this information to help determine model types and numbers of lags to use, as shown in the following:

- AR models will have an ACF that slowly diminishes or cycles, and its PACF will cut off under a significance line after a certain number of lags
- MA models will have a PACF that slowly diminishes or cycles, and its ACF will cut off under a significance line after a certain number of lags

Data for *AR(2)* and *MA(1)* time series were simulated to demonstrate these plots. The ACF and PACF plots for AR and MA models are shown in the following diagram:

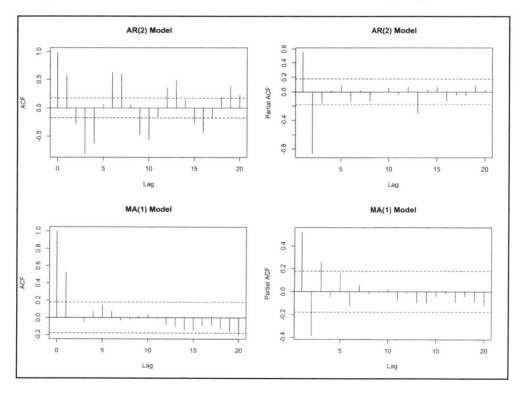

Notice how AR has a very cyclical ACF and the PACF cuts off after two lags (by the way, in this R package, the PACF starts at one and not zero). When you see a lag randomly pop up, such as at lag 13 in the AR(2) PACF, know that you can expect a random lag to appear in every 20 lags using a statistical significance value of 0.05.

Meanwhile, the MA model shows a cyclical PACF and the ACF cuts off after one lag. These models present similar plots. It can be difficult to tell the difference if you do not know the model, as we did in this simulation. You see some similarities, yet they are different. Having an idea of the model type and lag, you will then build and fit models.

One other useful tool is the plot generated by the `tsdiag()` function. You will apply this to an ARIMA model that already fits the data. It provides a view of standardized residuals (which should be random), an ACF plot (with a cut off at zero), and p-values (which should be above the critical point given as a dashed line). Here is a `tsdiag()` plot for the *AR(2)*:

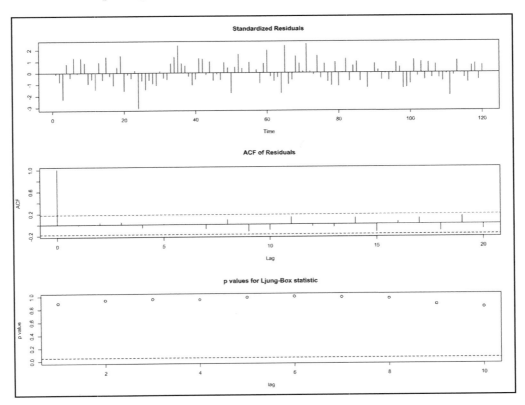

This plot provides an example of a good diagnostic result. Now you will work on the ridership use case. First, a review of the key steps that you could perform is as follows:

1. Convert your data into a time series data type, adapting your data as needed.
2. Inspect the time series with the `decompose()` function.
3. If data is non-stationary, try differencing to see if it helps to make it stationary.
4. Determine the ARIMA model type and lags for the non-seasonal component.
5. Model different options and determine the best fit based on diagnostics.
6. Determine the ARIMA model type and lags for the seasonal component.
7. Model different options and determine the best fit based on diagnostics.
8. Generate a forecast for the desired number of periods into the future.

Begin by loading the data and use the `head()` function on the ridership data:

```
cycle <- read.csv("./data/Ch6_ridership_data_2011-2012.csv")
head(cycle)
```

We will get the following output:

```
            datetime count
1 2011-01-01 00:00:00    16
2 2011-01-01 01:00:00    40
3 2011-01-01 02:00:00    32
4 2011-01-01 03:00:00    13
5 2011-01-01 04:00:00     1
6 2011-01-01 05:00:00     1
```

The finance group asked you to aggregate the data on a monthly basis so that forecasts from the model provide monthly periods. The `dplyr` and `lubridate` packages are good tools to aggregate data. Using them reinforces skills you learned earlier in this book:

```
library(dplyr); library(lubridate)
monthly_ride <- as.data.frame(cycle %>%
        group_by(year = year(datetime), month = month(datetime)) %>%
        summarise(riders = sum(count)))
```

A quality check using `table(monthly_ride$year, monthly_ride$month)` shows that the aggregation resulted in a single value for each month in both years-a good output:

```
     1 2 3 4 5 6 7 8 9 10 11 12
2011 1 1 1 1 1 1 1 1 1  1  1  1
2012 1 1 1 1 1 1 1 1 1  1  1  1
```

This data is still not a time series until you convert it. You have converted data before, for instance, from characters into time. The data is first subset to get a single column from the data frame. Then, you will create the time series using the `ts()` function:

```
riders <- monthly_ride[ ,3]
monthly <- ts(riders, frequency = 12, start = c(2011, 1))
```

The `frequency` parameter is set to `12` as you have twelve data points (months) in every period (one year). The `start` parameter indicates that the first data point is the first month of 2011. View the time series to see that the data is loaded properly:

```
> monthly
       Jan    Feb    Mar    Apr    May    Jun    Jul    Aug    Sep    Oct    Nov    Dec
2011 37727  46396  65109  90332 132580 139674 147426 134280 116825 120535 106361  84025
2012 94832 101668 158535 176349 195114 204683 196014 209024 208995 191108 158855 133735
```

This finishes Step 1. Now, run `plot(decompose(monthly))` to inspect the time series. You will see the original data at the top, an increasing trend line, and some regular seasonality. The bottom panel shows leftover errors, as follows:

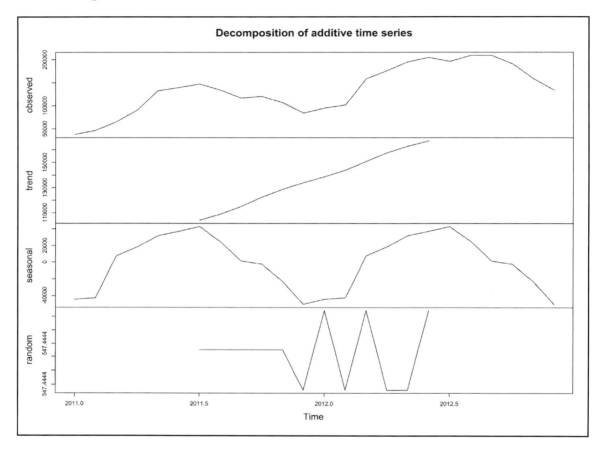

Step 3 is to run the differencing to see how to make the data stationary. Here are plots showing the original data, differencing, and seasonal differencing:

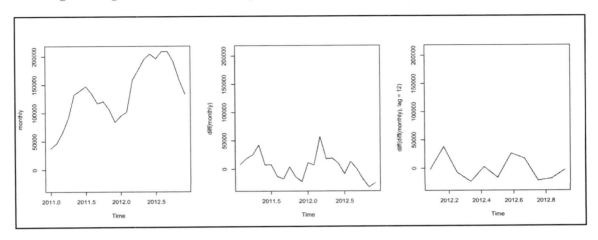

In this case, differencing eliminates the trend and makes the data stationary. The seasonal differencing does not appear to make the data any more stationary. This may seem surprising, but differencing of the non-seasonal component is sufficient.

Moving to Step 4, generate ACF and PACF plots to get a sense of types and levels of models you may want to fit in this monthly data:

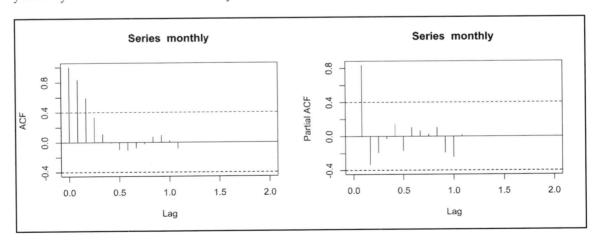

These plots look different from the earlier plots. There are very few lags. Yes, you are seeing them all, but there are only a few as the dataset contains only two years of data. Two data points from each cycle are typically the minimum amount of data to fit a time series model properly. Think about this, would you try to predict a linear model based on two data points? In time series, two complete periods only provide two observations for each part of the cycle. Both points better be perfect, otherwise your model will be very poor in forecasting the next point. We will continue, but be aware, you may see poor forecasting.

BI tip: Most organizations have plenty of time-based data available for analysis. Economic analysis is popular and your business colleagues will likely understand the implications of using too little data for time series analysis.

The plots show a slowly-diminishing ACF turning into a cycle. This is a clue that the data is AR. The PACF cuts off within the first lag. This would point you towards an *AR(1)* model with no seasonal component (based on the differencing results).

Step 5 is quite easy. Fit a number of models and then compare their results, including **Akaike Information Criterion (AIC)** (lower is better), and diagnostic plots. You may decide to create five models: two *AR(1)* models with and without differencing, one *AR(2)* with differencing, one *AR(1)* with differencing and seasonal differencing, and one *MA(1)* with differencing. You will fit ARIMA models using this general form, replacing the letters with values:

```
model_name <- arima(data, c(p, d, q),
                    seasonal = list(order = c(P, D, Q)))
```

The following code creates the fitted models and generates tabular output and diagnostic plots:

```
fit1 <- arima(monthly, c(1, 0, 0),
          seasonal = list(order = c(0, 0, 0)))
fit1; tsdiag(fit1)

fit2 <- arima(monthly, c(1, 1, 0),
          seasonal = list(order = c(0, 0, 0)))
fit2; tsdiag(fit2)

fit3 <- arima(monthly, c(2, 1, 0),
          seasonal = list(order = c(0, 0, 0)))
fit3; tsdiag(fit3)

fit4 <- arima(monthly, c(1, 1, 0),
```

```
                  seasonal = list(order = c(0, 1, 0)))
fit4; tsdiag(fit4)

fit5 <- arima(monthly, c(0, 1, 1),
                  seasonal = list(order = c(0, 0, 0)))
fit5; tsdiag(fit5)
```

Here are the results of five different models to compare AIC and diagnostics:

Model	AIC	Diagnostics
ARIMA(1,0,0)(0,0,0)	553.74	Poor residuals and poor p-values
ARIMA(1,1,0)(0,0,0)	520.96	Good diagnostics
ARIMA(2,1,0)(0,0,0)	522.63	Good diagnostics
ARIMA(1,1,0)(0,1,0)	252.38	Poor p-values
ARIMA(0,1,1)(0,0,0)	523.30	Poor p-values

The second model is *AR(1)* with differencing. It is simpler than *AR(2)* and provides slightly better AIC. Now, you will run the `forecast()` function found in the `forecast` package to use the fitted *AR(1)* model and `h = 12` for the next 12 data points (months):

```
library(forecast)
yr_forecast <- forecast(fit2, h = 12)
plot(yr_forecast)
```

The output we get is shown in the following diagram:

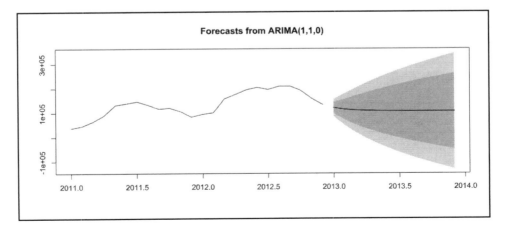

The blue line in the center represents the mean forecast. The dark inner cone represents the 80% interval. The light outer cone represents the 90% forecast interval. Not a pretty forecast. It communicates the message that *anything is possible: growth, loss, or flat year*. This is too general to be of much use to the business. The trouble with this forecast is that the methods do not work on small trends such as this. Advanced techniques can help.

Learn more: You have just worked through a lot of information. Do not feel bad if this is all new and a little mystical. Remember that the intent is to give you an exposure to these methods and not deep knowledge. Also, remember that it is better to be aware of a little than to be completely uninformed just because it is a challenging technique.

If you found this section interesting, you may be ready to learn more about the topic from a university perspective. Refer to the **Welcome to STAT 510 – Applied Time Series Analysis** online course. It is freely available at `https://onlinecourses.science.psu.edu/stat51/node/3` `3`.

Using advanced functionality for modeling

This section is short and exposes you to the fact that advanced techniques exist to help with complex time series modeling. Remember that time series analysis is a type of regression. The ridership data contained only two years of data. That is hardly enough to build a reliable forecast for the next year that included seasonality. Perhaps if you had ten years of data, you could model the seasonality and get a more trustworthy forecast.

Advanced functions exist that work with smaller data sets such as your ridership data. The `tbats` package performs high-level mathematics, such as Fourier transforms, to fit models with smaller data. This technique also works well when your `frequency` parameter exceeds 24 (used for hourly aggregations). The `arima()` function cannot work with frequencies such as 52, which you may want if your model is based on weekly aggregations over a year. To run the advanced function, you call the `tbats()` function on the data:

```
monthly_data <- tbats(monthly)
```

Yes, it is very simple to run the `tbats()` function. You now have a fitted model. Use it to create a forecast for the next year:

```
year_forecast <- forecast(monthly_data, h = 12)
plot(year_forecast)
```

We will get the following output:

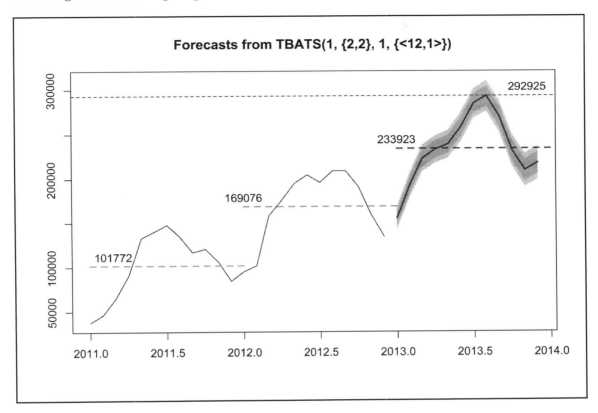

Forecasts from TBATS(1, {2,2}, 1, {<12,1>})

R tip: Do not allow the simplicity of this technique to fool you. Be respectful of its power and use it wisely while making forecasts. This technique appears in this book only after investigating a number of methods. TBATS worked with this particular dataset, but it may not work well with other short time series.

There are many other advanced techniques. You can read about them in Rob Hyndman's blog. He does a very good job at explaining R techniques for time series analysis in understandable terms. You can find many approaches at `http://robjhyndman.com/hyndsight/`.

The forecast in the plot looks reasonable. The middle parameters in the title, **{2,2}**, indicate this has an *AR(2)* and *MA(2)* component. The other parameters are specific to the method. The forecast shows a trend and seasonality comparable to the data you have. From the business perspective, you can expect questions about this forecast. These may include:

- What is the maximum ridership level for next year?
- What is the average ridership level for next year?
- How do both values compare to the historical data?

This plot anticipated these questions and added information to the basic plot. Like other modeling objects, you can extract this information from the fitted model. Begin with summaries to get an idea of the available information.

First, get a summary of the average:

```
summary(year_forecast$mean)
```

The output is as follows:

```
   Min. 1st Qu.  Median    Mean 3rd Qu.    Max.
 155300  215900  232300  233900  260900  292900
```

Then, summarize the upper end of the forecast interval:

```
summary(year_forecast$upper)
```

The following is the output:

```
      V1                    V2
 Min.   :164108     Min.   :168788
 1st Qu.:228134     1st Qu.:234617
 Median :243134     Median :248848
 Mean   :244606     Mean   :250262
 3rd Qu.:271888     3rd Qu.:277705
 Max.   :304163     Max.   :310112
```

Lastly, take a look at the lower end of the forecast interval:

```
summary(year_forecast$lower)
```

The output is as shown here:

```
         V1                   V2
 Min.    :146425    Min.    :141745
 1st Qu.:203639     1st Qu.:197155
 Median :221544     Median :215830
 Mean    :223240    Mean    :217585
 3rd Qu.:249914     3rd Qu.:244098
 Max.    :281688    Max.    :275739
```

These summaries show you the data available to extract in order to accent the plot. The following is the code snippet used to create the annotations. Begin by getting the yearly means and maximum ridership:

```
mean_2011 <- round(as.numeric(filter(monthly_ride, year == 2011) %>%
          summarise(mean = mean(riders))), 0)
mean_2012 <- round(as.numeric(filter(monthly_ride, year == 2012) %>%
          summarise(mean = mean(riders))), 0)
mean_2013 <- round(mean(year_forecast$mean), 0)
max_mean_2013 <- round(max(year_forecast$mean), 0)
```

Now use the variables to create a top line representing the maximum of the mean forecast, as well as segments that span across only the individual years to show the mean for each year:

```
abline(h = max(year_forecast$mean), lty = 2, col = "blue")
segments(2011, mean_2011, x1 = 2012, y1 = mean_2011,
        col = "darkgray", lty = 2, lwd = 2)
segments(2012, mean_2012, x1 = 2013, y1 = mean_2012,
        col = "darkgray", lty = 2, lwd = 2)
segments(2013, mean_2013, x1 = 2014, y1 = mean_2013,
        col = "blue", lty = 2, lwd = 2)
```

Finally, label each of the lines and segments with the mean values that you can extract from the fitted model. You use the `text()` function and pass it the x and y coordinates, followed by the text you would like on the plot. In this case, you will also pass the text as a variable. Adding `10000` to the y coordinate lifts it off the line for readability:

```
text(2011.15, mean_2011 + 10000, mean_2011)
text(2012, mean_2012 + 10000, mean_2012)
text(2013, mean_2013 + 10000, mean_2013)
text(2013.85, max_mean_2013 + 10000, max_mean_2013)
```

You did it. Congratulations! You were able to work with a small dataset and produce a data-centric product that gives the finance group an idea about the ridership next year, along with 80% and 90% confidence levels. By adding the advanced Fourier transforms found in the `tbats` package, you were able to provide a sense of volume as well as timing of the ridership through the months.

Things are looking good at Bike Sharing LLC. The company can anticipate a solid year with over 35% growth in average ridership, and the peak monthly ridership could grow 40% over last year.

Summary

Congratulations, you truly deserve recognition for getting through a very tough topic. You now have more awareness about time series analysis than some people with formal statistical training. You learned first-hand why linear regression is inappropriate for data that violates the assumption of independence. For time series (dependent) data, there is an assumption that the data is stationary. When the data does not meet this assumption, you can apply techniques such as differencing to help make it stationary. The R software includes specialized tools to create, inspect, and even decompose time-based data. This provided you with clues as you learned about the ARIMA model, which is a combination of three different modeling techniques applied simultaneously. These techniques, similar to other models, require both art and science in their use. Additionally, you can apply the ARIMA model to non-seasonal and seasonal components, when both exist. Finally, you learned that you must have enough historical data to make good forecasts. Advanced techniques and good resources help when you encounter problems associated with small datasets.

This chapter ends the second part of this book and concludes your learning about analysis techniques. The third part contains two chapters to help you communicate the results of your analysis. Specifically, in the next chapter, you will look at different tools available in R to help you visualize data and results.

7
Visualizing the Data's Story

"When you tell a story, people lean in; when you start talking about data, their eyes glaze over."

— Eshelman-Haynes, Gendron, S. Hall, & B. Hall (2016)

The data you analyze has a story to tell, and your future as a data storyteller is as limitless as your imagination. **Visualization** is the act of transforming the complexity of numbers into a picture that tells a story. This chapter touches on the intersections between art and analysis. We will look at the following four topics to introduce this relationship:

- Visualizing data
- Plotting with `ggplot2`
- Geo-mapping using Leaflet
- Creating interactive graphics using `rCharts`

Your tools will include your imagination and a wide array of R packages designed to help you produce stunning visualizations. We cannot cover the syntax and logic of each package in detail, so consider this chapter a starting point. Begin your exploration of data visualization in R with this guide and continue to develop your style by paying attention to the visual designs you find appealing. Ask yourself questions such as: what makes them appealing? Why are they powerful? How can I adapt the design elements into my work?

Visualizing data

Your journey into the world of visualization starts with this observation-numbers are explicit and objective, visuals are implicit and subjective. Hidden within the numbers, shapes, and colors is a message that is subject to the interpretation of the viewer. Realize what happens as the visual image transforms through our senses into an understanding.

The brain will subconsciously pass judgement in determining what information is essential and what is supportive. Sight becomes perception. Perception becomes cognition and knowledge (*Cairo, 2013*).

Calling attention to information

If sight is perception, then data storytellers must consider how to use visual elements to call attention to the most critical information. According to *Cairo (2013)*, *The brain is much better at quickly detecting shade variations than shape differences (p. 113)*. He provides tips on how to call the user's attention to particular portions of a visual. First, he suggests using pure colors to highlight the most relevant information. Second, use subdued hues to present a bulk of the remaining data. Subdued hues include grays, light blues, and many shades of green. These colors are abundant in nature-surrounding colors.

Despite these guidelines, *Cairo (2011)* comments on the duality of color: although it can grab a user's attention, it is a difficult element to facilitate decision-making. People interpret certain colors differently. However, color is only one tool in our visualization toolbox. *Cairo* thinks of the visual elements such as lines and shapes as a spectrum:

- Position along a common scale
- Length, direction, or angle
- Area
- Volume or curvature
- Shading or color saturation

The elements at the top of the list are useful when the information requires accurate judgment. Those toward the bottom capture ones attention more easily. Use combinations of these elements to capture the user's attention and provide better insights to the detail that your visualizations should convey.

Empowering user interpretation

Shneiderman (1996) is a well-regarded leader in information visualization. Over many projects, he identified patterns in visual design success. This led him to capture the basic principles of the **Visual Information-Seeking Mantra**. It is simply stated as follows:

> *"Overview first, zoom and filter, then details-on-demand."*
>
> – *Ben Shneiderman*

His mantra can help you remember the following three basic steps to develop visualization flow:

- **Overview** gives users a sense of the dataset. The entire dataset.
- **Zoom and Filter** allow users to zoom-in on things that interest them, as well as filter out those things that do not.
- **Details-on-demand** allow users to select an item or groups of items to delve into greater detail as they desire.

Remember these items as we develop visualizations in this chapter to communicate data. Have fun and explore. As *Cairo* instructs us, *Experimenting (carefully) with novel forms is not just a whimsical impulse, it's a necessity* (2013, p. 85).

Plotting with ggplot2

Wilkinson (2005) developed *The Grammar of Graphics* as a way of approaching data visualization by describing them as individual components working together. *Wickham* (2010) used this grammar to develop the `ggplot2` package. In `ggplot2`, you can create plots by adding each component of the visualization as a layer. In this section, you will recreate a scatterplot from `Chapter 4`, *Linear Regression for Business* that you built using base R graphics. Convert `emp_size` to a factor to see its effect in visualizing information:

```
plot_dat <- read.csv("./data/Ch7_marketing.csv")
plot_dat$emp_size <- cut(plot_dat$employees, breaks = 3,
        labels = c("Employees: 3 - 6", "7 - 9", "10+"))
library(ggplot2); library(scales)
plot <- ggplot(data = plot_dat, aes(x = marketing_total,
            y = revenues))
```

First, you will use the `ggplot()` function to create a basic plot object and pass it the `plot_dat` dataset. Note that the command will not actually produce a plot. It only sets up the basic plot information: an x-axis for the marketing expenditures and y-axis for the revenue. With this basic plot, you can add layers such as the points, labeling, and formatting. These layers will produce the plot you envision. Layers are added using the + operator:

```
plot <- plot + facet_grid(. ~ emp_size) +
    geom_point(aes(color = pop_density), shape = 18, size = 4)
```

You would like to separate the data points into columnar panels based on the `emp_size` factor. The `facet_grid()` function creates that effect. Meanwhile, the `geom_point()` function adds a `geom` layer to represent the data points, as well as an aesthetic for color based on the `pop_density` variable, a shape, and a size. The plot still needs more layers as it would not be complete without proper axis labelling and formatting:

```
plot + scale_y_continuous(labels = dollar,
                          breaks = pretty_breaks(n = 5)) +
     scale_x_continuous(labels = dollar,
                        breaks = pretty_breaks(n = 5)) +
     scale_color_discrete(guide = guide_legend(
                          title = "Population\nDensity")) +
     xlab("Marketing Expenditures ($K)") + ylab("Revenues ($K)")
```

The `scale_y_continuous()` and `scales_x_continuous()` functions allow you to format the axes with labels in the *dollar* format and with five nicely spaced major gridlines.

R tip: Creating a simple plot is usually only half the battle, the other half is styling it. We recommend that you use the `scales` package with `ggplot2` as it provides convenient functions such as `dollar()` and `pretty_breaks()` to make it easier to style charts in a more professional and presentable manner.

The `scale_color_discrete()` function provides access to format the legend with a more informative title. Finally, the `xlab()` and `ylab()` functions allow you to layer in the axis labels:

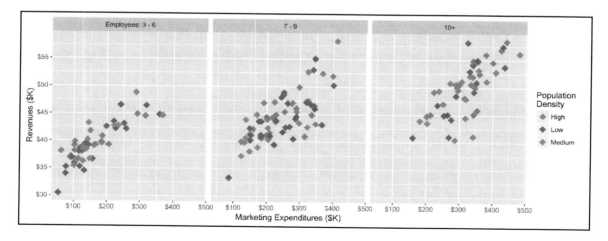

There is a lot of functionality in the ggplot2 package and much more to learn.

Learn more: The `ggplot2` package is as amazing as it is comprehensive. You can learn a lot about the various layers and practice with your own datasets by starting with this helpful cheat sheet at `http://www.rstudio.com/wp-content/uploads/2015/12/ggplot2-cheats heet-2.0.pdf`.

Geo-mapping using Leaflet

Geo-mapping is the process of placing markers representing data in a geographic context, typically using latitude and longitude. Leaflet is an open source JavaScript library for building interactive geo-maps with ease. Why are we talking about a JavaScript mapping library in an R book? The R package `leaflet` is a wrapper around this JavaScript library that translates most of its functionality into a set of R functions. It allows analysts to visualize geospatial data easily. With this package, you can generate maps from within RStudio or embed them in R Markdown documents or Shiny web applications.

Use case: Geo-mapping Bike Stations

Remember when you supported management by creating a business case for the location of customer service kiosks? You had data on each of the 244 Bike Sharing stations throughout the city. Go ahead and pull this same data from the file called `Ch7_bike_station_locations.csv`, located on the book's website at `http://jgendron.github.io/com.packtpub.intro .r.bi/`. Now you will depict these same locations using geo-mapping techniques.

Learning geo-mapping

Geo-mapping allows for more than just identifying locations. Think of how one of your favorite mobile apps utilizes a map view. The map most likely includes layers of detailed information and popups with data, such as business description, hours of operation, or customer ratings.

Learn more: The `leaflet` package makes extensive use of a special operator called the forward pipe operator, `%>%`. The operator takes input on the left-hand side and pushes it through to another operation waiting on the right-hand side of `%>%`. You can learn more about the `%>%` operator by visiting Stefan Milton Bache's tutorial on the CRAN website at `https://cran.r-project.org/web/packages/magrittr/vignettes/magrittr.html`.

To explore the `leaflet` package, read in the bike station locations data file and examine it. You should be familiar with it. Two columns provide the latitude and longitude coordinates of each Bike Sharing station:

```
stations <- read.csv("./data/Ch7_bike_station_locations.csv")
library(magrittr); library(leaflet)
```

The power of the `leaflet` package is that you can generate an interactive map of these station locations with only three lines of R code:

```
leaflet() %>%
    addTiles() %>%
    addMarkers(data = stations, ~longitude, ~latitude)
```

The following is the output:

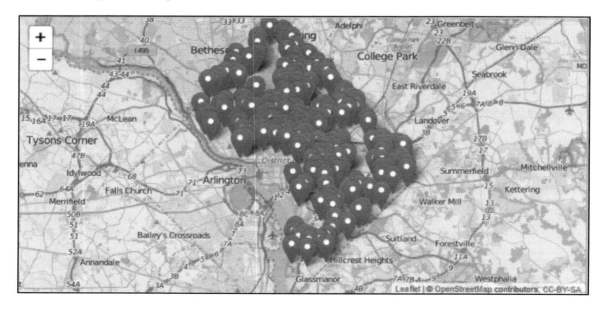

These three lines of R code can be broken down into the following logic:

- The `leaflet()` function creates a blank canvas that is map-ready
- The forward pipe operator takes this map and passes it the `addTiles()` function, which adds a backdrop to the map (showing streets and boundaries)
- Then, passing the map to the `addMarkers()` function puts a pin at each latitude and longitude coordinate provided by the `stations` data frame

If you prefer to change the default map tile or default markers, then the `leaflet` package makes it very easy to customize your solution. The following are the ways to customize a basic map that you just created:

- Changing the marker icon: Use any image file you would like and pass it to `addMarkers()` using the `makeIcon()` function to display it:

```
bike <- makeIcon("./data/bike.png", iconWidth = 20,
                 iconHeight = 20)
```

- Adding popups: Provide any details you would like about individual markers by passing information as a parameter to the `addMarkers()` function. It activates a popup with details-on-demand after clicking on a marker:

```
stations$popup <- paste0("Station Location #",
                         seq(1, nrow(stations)))
```

- Changing map background tiles: Use any available maps by passing a URL of a hosted tile in the `urlTemplate =` parameter:

```
new_tile_url <- "http://{s}.basemaps.cartocdn.
com/light_all/{z}/{x}/{y}.png"
new_tile_attribution_string <- '&copy;
    <a href="http://www.openstreetmap.org/copyright">
    OpenStreetMap</a>&copy;
    <a href="http://cartodb.com/attributions">CartoDB</a>'
```

Learn more: If no arguments are passed to the `addTiles()` function, then the default map tile is based on OpenStreetMap. There is an entire gallery of map tiles available. You can see a complete gallery of options at `http://leaflet-extras.github.io/leaflet-providers/preview/`. Each map contains URL and attribution strings that you simply paste into your R code, as shown above. Make sure that you give the map author credit by including the attribution string for the tile.

Now you can use all three of these customized elements by augmenting the code you created to regenerate the basic plot, but as a custom version that you can call your own:

```
leaflet() %>%
    addTiles(urlTemplate = new_tile_url,
             attribution = new_tile_attribution_string,
             options = providerTileOptions(noWrap = TRUE)) %>%
    addMarkers(data = stations, lng = ~longitude, lat = ~latitude,
               popup = ~popup, icon = bike)
```

BI tip: Business analysts want interactive data products and dashboards. Consider click actions when you are finalizing your datasets. It is best practice to include a column in your dataset that contains a pop-up message to display when a user clicks on a particular marker. The pop-up message can provide a wealth of information at a single click so that users do not need to go searching for data details in another location. Remember the mantra: details-on-demand.

Extending geo-mapping functionality

The `leaflet` package is useful for a wide range of projects that require attractive visualizations of geospatial data. Imagine that you are a business analyst who is working with the operations group at Bike Sharing LLC. Each week, a maintenance crew must travel to all of the bike stations in the city to perform routine maintenance activities. Budgets only allow one truck to service the entire city. The question is, *What is the optimal route that the truck should travel to visit all locations without wasting time and fuel?*

The task may seem daunting, but we can borrow the solution from a well-documented and classic optimization puzzle-the **Traveling Salesman Problem** (**TSP**). This problem mirrors your maintenance crew problem as it solves an optimal route for a salesperson to travel to each city in their region without passing through any city twice. One of the many benefits of using R is that there is a specific package called `TSP` to solve this type of optimization problem. Then, we can easily visualize the solution using Leaflet's geo-mapping capabilities.

Solving a TSP: The focus of this Leaflet example is geo-mapping a TSP solution. The TSP solution itself was developed, but not explicitly included in this book, as we wanted to focus on the visualization of the solution. However, fully-commented code demonstrating a TSP solution to the maintenance truck problem is available for you to explore and learn at
`https://github.com/jgendron/com.packtpub.intro.r.bi/tree/master/Chapter7-DataVisualization/TravelingSalesmanProblem`.

Assuming that we have a solution for an optimal truck route from the `TSP` package, we can read it as a data frame recorded in latitude and longitude coordinates:

```
short_path <- read.csv("./data/Ch7_optimal_maint_route.csv")
head(short_path)
```

We will get the output as follows:

```
  latitude longitude                popup
1 38.94950 -77.09362    Station Location #5
2 38.94899 -77.09976 Station Location #133
3 38.93447 -77.08431 Station Location #115
4 38.93154 -77.08812 Station Location #217
5 38.93195 -77.10650   Station Location #80
6 38.92521 -77.10285 Station Location #124
```

Let us see the following code:

```
nrow(short_path)
```

It will return the output as follows:

```
[1] 243
```

The shortest path contains 243 segments spanning the 244 bike station locations. You can use `leaflet` to geo-map the solution with a code very similar to the previous example:

```
leaflet() %>%
    addTiles() %>%
    addCircleMarkers(data = short_path, lat = ~latitude,
                     lng = ~longitude, radius = 3,
                     popup = ~popup) %>%
    addPolylines(data = short_path, lat = ~latitude,
                 lng = ~longitude, color = "#A93E36",
                 opacity = .7)
```

The output is as shown in the following:

Notice that you used another function from the `leaflet` package called `addPolylines()`. This function provides a straight line between points on our map to depict the optimal path for the service truck.

R tip: Take advantage of the various parameters available in R functions. Passing values to `color` and `opacity` allows you to refine the plotted path on the map and provide visual contrast between the data and geographic backdrop to see the essence of your message more clearly.

Congratulations! The operations group liked your solution. It was a very impressive use of geo-mapping. You used the power of visualizing the data to tell its story. They tested the solution and found it was 50% more efficient than the previous attempts to service the bike stations.

This is just a single use case for geo-mapping. It leveraged one of the rich libraries available in R to solve an optimization problem and allowed you to communicate this solution by visualizing the results to demonstrate business value.

Creating interactive graphics using rCharts

The R implementation of the Leaflet JavaScript library is just one of many JavaScript visualization libraries translated into R. The popularity of JavaScript charting frameworks has risen because major media outlets and blogging sites have started focusing the content around awe-inspiring graphics. As these graphics enter mainstream media, this poses a question you should consider: *How can I visualize my own data in new and different ways that are more appropriate for the questions I am trying to answer?*

> **Use case: Communicating E-mail Campaign Success**
> As you can imagine, marketing the Bike Sharing brand means getting the word out about the business. E-mail marketing campaigns can encourage individuals to sign up for memberships through the Bike Sharing website. The marketing team has tried an A/B testing strategy of the following two types of promotional e-mail offers:
>
>
>
> * Getting 10% off a yearly membership
> * Giving the first month free
>
> They would like your help to know which strategy is more effective. One way to determine the effectiveness is to keep track of a recipient's click trail from opening the e-mail, to clicking on the link, to creating an account, and hopefully signing up for membership. Each of these steps has a conversion rate, where a portion of people will move to the next step in the process. The IT staff has logged the events and provided a dataset that you can use in your analysis. The `Ch7_email_marketing_campaign.csv` dataset is located on the book's website at `http://jgendron.github.io/com.packtpub.intro.r.bi/`. Now, get ready for some interesting visualization work!

Framing the data story

Before creating more complex or specialized data visualizations, remember that you are telling a story. Begin by framing the question at hand and sketching out the elements of the message you want to communicate. You can use a simple approach such as pencil and paper. Another approach is to use R base graphics or the `ggplot2` package to develop a prototype. Either approach provides a process to give you an understanding of what a visual could look like and determine whether you have the data points available to create the chart.

R tip: You can find many other packages to help you with your visualization work. Here are just a few examples:

- `dygraphs`: This is to chart time series and the evolution of a process over time
- `networkD3`: This is to visualize networks, trees, dendrograms, and Sankey graphs
- `DiagrammeR`: This is to create graph diagrams (edges and nodes) and flowcharts
- `rCharts`: This is to create interactive and engaging versions of common chart types

The purpose of listing a variety of packages is to show how important the world of graphics and visualization has become. As specialty packages continue to arrive, know that the right tool for one job might not be the best one for another project. Our recommendation is that you not only review the R package documentation, but also go to the JavaScript library documentation to understand how to extend the core functionality.

Learn more: A team of individuals supporting the `htmlwidgets` package continues to create a growing body of work in the visualization arena. Their work in translating these types of graphics into R has a very broad scope and you can learn more at `http://www.htmlwidgets.org/`.

Learning interactive graphing with JavaScript

As usual, read the dataset into R and look at the content:

```
dat <- read.csv("./data/Ch7_email_marketing_campaign.csv",
                check.names = FALSE)
head(dat)
```

The output is shown here:

Consumer	Promotion	Opened Email	Clicked Email Link	Created Account	Paid for Membership
1	1 Free Month	N	N	N	N
2	2 10% off	N	N	N	N
3	3 Free Month	N	N	N	N
4	4 10% off	N	N	N	N
5	5 Free Month	N	N	N	N
6	6 10% off	N	N	N	N

The last four columns track recipient click actions (coded as Y or N). This data is human-readable, but it is not in a format that the machine can manipulate. You will need to aggregate the counts of each event by the type of promotion. This requires you to create a row (observation) containing Promotion, click Event type, and Outcome for each action. The reshape2 package provides the melt() function that restructures the data.

The following code takes the dat data frame and subsets the last five columns. Then it specifies the shape using the id.vars, variable.name, and value.name parameters:

```
library(reshape2)
dat2 <- melt(dat[, 2:6], id.vars = "Promotion",
             variable.name = "Event", value.name = "Outcome")
head(dat2)
```

The output is as follows:

```
    Promotion        Event Outcome
1 Free Month Opened Email       N
2    10% off Opened Email       N
3 Free Month Opened Email       N
4    10% off Opened Email       N
5 Free Month Opened Email       N
6    10% off Opened Email       N
```

After reshaping the data, we can recode the outcomes as 0's and 1's in order to aggregate by promotion and event, and count the number of successes under each combination:

```
dat2$Outcome <- ifelse(dat2$Outcome == "Y", 1, 0)
aggregate <- aggregate(Outcome ~ Promotion + Event, FUN = sum,
                       data = dat2)
aggregate
```

The following is the output:

```
  Promotion            Event Outcome
1   10% off      Opened Email     308
2 Free Month      Opened Email     388
3   10% off Clicked Email Link     143
4 Free Month Clicked Email Link     194
5   10% off   Created Account     115
6 Free Month   Created Account     114
7   10% off Paid for Membership     106
8 Free Month Paid for Membership      83
```

This aggregation already reveals interesting patterns in the data. More people opened the `Free Month` e-mail, but fewer signed up for a paid membership compared to the `10% off` promotion. A visualization would help tell this story.

The `rCharts` package provides a `multiBarChart` interactive visualization that allows users to explore the data for themselves. Do you remember the second element of Shneiderman's mantra to zoom and filter? The `aggregate` data frame contains all the data points to create a bar for each promotion and event. Refer to `Appendix C`, *R Packages Used in the Book* for instructions to install `rCharts`:

```
library(rCharts)
n1 <- nPlot(Outcome ~ Event, group = "Promotion",
            data = aggregate, type = "multiBarChart")
```

This simple line of code creates a powerful chart. Each of the promotion types is clickable to toggle their display and you can toggle between grouped and stacked bar chart types.

 Learn more: For most chart types in the rCharts package, you can add the components of the chart incrementally and then plot them. It is a fair question to ask, *Where can I find information on the various parameters? They are not documented in R help.* As mentioned earlier, it is often better to use the JavaScript documentation to learn the potential options for configuration.

The multiBarChart from the rCharts package is an implementation from the NVD3 JavaScript library, so the supported configuration options will be almost exactly what the NVD3 documentation outlines at https://nvd3-community.github.io/nvd3/examples/documentation.html. Even with the documented JavaScript functionality, a description of its use in an R package might not exist. It is a best practice to approach charting with a try-and-see attitude.

These features essentially provide four different charts all in one visualization! Now, you can enhance the chart with some styling and annotations:

```
n1$xAxis(axisLabel = "Event Type", staggerLabels = FALSE,
        rotateLabels = 0)
n1$yAxis(axisLabel = "Conversions", width = 40,
        tickFormat = "#! d3.format('.0f') !#",
        showMaxMin = TRUE)
n1$chart(color = c("#006CB8", "#ED1C24"))
n1$params$width <- 700
n1$params$height <- 400
n1
```

We will get the output as follows:

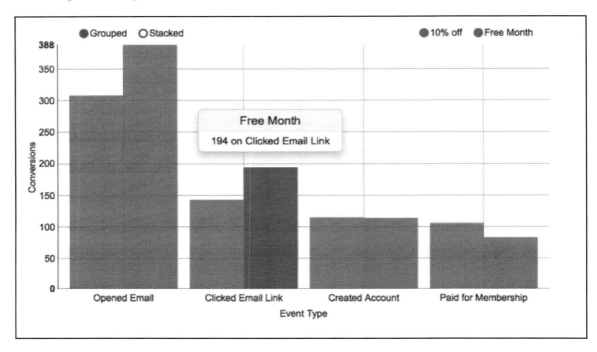

The bar chart is interesting, but a Sankey diagram might yield a better way to visualize the conversion rates in a process flow. Sankey diagramming tools require the data to be in a particular format. You must identify the source and target of each flow, as well as a value. In our case, an example source would be Sent Email and the target would be Opened Email or No Action. The Opened Email source would then have two possible targets, Clicked on Email Link or No Action. The other events will have a similar structure. The dataset for the Sankey diagram exists on the website where you have found the other datasets at http://jgendron.github.io/com.packtpub.intro.r.bi/:

```
dat <- read.csv("./data/Ch7_email_marketing_conversions.csv",
                check.names = FALSE)
head(dat)
```

We will get the output as follows:

```
    Promotion         Source              Target Count   Percent
1 Free Month     Sent Email       Opened Email    388 0.388000
2    10% off     Sent Email       Opened Email    308 0.308000
3 Free Month     Sent Email          No Action    612 0.612000
4    10% off     Sent Email          No Action    692 0.692000
5 Free Month   Opened Email Clicked Email Link    194 0.500000
6    10% off   Opened Email Clicked Email Link    143 0.464286
```

The structure of this dataset has already been prepared for creating a Sankey diagram. We can examine the 10% off promotion by subsetting the data and renaming the columns according to the package Sankey plot requirements-source, target, and value:

```
promotion1 <- dat[dat$Promotion == "10% off", 2:4]
colnames(promotion1) <- c("source", "target", "value")
sankeyPlot <- rCharts$new()
sankeyPlot$setLib("http://timelyportfolio.github.io/rCharts_d3_sankey/libra
ries/widgets/d3_sankey")
sankeyPlot$set(
    data = promotion1,
    nodeWidth = 25,
    nodePadding = 100,
    layout = 800,
    width = 700,
    height = 500
)
sankeyPlot
```

The output is as follows:

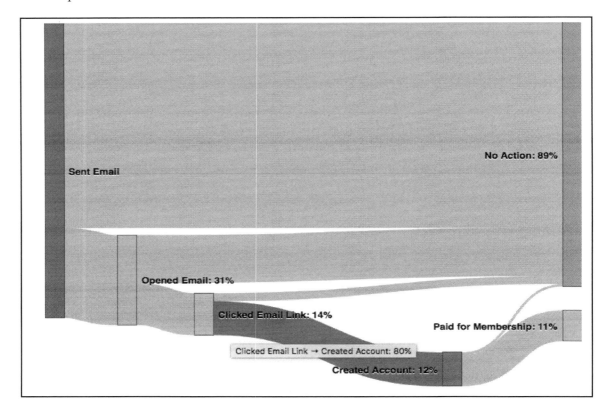

When you run the preceding code, you might notice that your visual is missing some elements (percentages at each node; the text is a little larger and bolder). This is because some extra styling and annotation were performed with the setTemplate() function.

Learn more: If you would like to reproduce the graphic exactly as pictured, the complete code is accessible at:
`https://github.com/jgendron/com.packtpub.intro.r.bi/blob/maste`
`r/Chapter7-DataVisualization/DataVisualization.R`.
It uses the setTemplate() function. When using JavaScript charts in R, the customization is still best when you use small snippets of native JavaScript.

Look at the visual. There is an interesting statistic: 80% of individuals who clicked on the e-mail link created an account. In contrast, the `Free Month` promotion had only 59% conversion from click to account creation. From the bar chart and Sankey diagrams, it appears more individuals opened the `Free Month` e-mail, but they just did not convert as well as the `10% off` promotion.

Good job on working through all the case studies and visualization frameworks. Your work really paid off as the marketing team understands e-mail conversion patterns better, the operations group is more efficient in performing maintenance, and the company has some better expectations on the returns of marketing expenditures.

Summary

The material in this chapter truly gave you a lot of information to absorb. We hope that you will explore the additional resources in the **Learn more** sections to continue building on the foundations covered in the sections. You learned about visualizing data from a cognitive perspective and underlying principles to creating visuals that catch someone's attention and help them interpret the data. The variety of packages presented showed you how to generate geo-mapping and charting projects. The use cases provided you with examples that were not only interesting for users to look at, but also interactive to help engage them. These interactive graphics can later become elements of online web pages, applications, or even dashboards because JavaScript is a Web-ready technology.

In the final chapter of this book, you will learn how to create a classic product of business intelligence-the dashboard. It will focus on the use of R's web application framework, called Shiny, as a tool to impress your decision makers with interactive and Web-based dashboarding.

8

Web Dashboards with Shiny

Insights gathered from data are great, but interactive web-based insights are even better. As a business analyst, you strive to transform analysis into actionable insights that solve business problems and drive change. Poorly communicated insights diminish the value of your data project. The shift towards web-based technologies to deliver information has put increasing pressure on business analysts to communicate results via the Web. Shiny is a web application framework for R that harnesses the power of modern web technologies. You can build sophisticated web applications using simple pieces of R code that you already know. This chapter will teach you the building blocks of a Shiny web app:

- Creating a basic Shiny app
- Creating a marketing-campaign Shiny app
- Deploying your Shiny app

Knowledge of web programming in HTML, CSS, or JavaScript is not required to develop Shiny apps; familiarity with them will help you understand Shiny and extend its core functionality. Building a Shiny app does not require you to be an expert R coder either; however, a working knowledge of the topics covered earlier in this book (loading data, cleaning data, and creating graphics) will accelerate your app development and allow you to focus on the core aspects of Shiny.

Use case: Advertising Revenue Prediction Tool

In `Chapter 4`, *Linear Regression for Business,* you created a linear regression model. Now you have an idea: the marketing group could really benefit from a web application to make revenue predictions based on the linear model you created. This would put analytical power in their hands. You have decided to create a Shiny app to show your boss. The book's website at `http://jgendron.github.io/com.packtpub.intro.r.bi/` contains the `Ch8_marketing.csv` data file. Enjoy this design process. The second Shiny app in this chapter introduces advanced features once you can build a basic Shiny app.

Creating a basic Shiny app

Shiny apps function within a specific folder and file structure. At a minimum, a Shiny app contains a user interface (client-side logic) and server-side logic. The **client-side logic** is the portion of the application that appears and functions in the user's Web browser. For example, a client-side feature of your app might be a slider bar used to input a value.

The **server-side logic** is any part of the application that executes on the web server hosting the application. For example, your app might receive the client-side slider bar value as an input to run a prediction from a linear model you developed and stored on the server. Recognizing this division between the client-side and server-side logic can help you understand the two files essential for a standard Shiny app:

- A `ui.R` file containing all the client-side logic
- A `server.R` file containing all the server-side logic

RStudio will automatically create `ui.R` and `server.R` files if you create a new project and choose **New Directory** and **Shiny Web Application** as the type. For this basic Shiny app, you will also create a `data` folder to hold the dataset that you will load into the app. Here is what your project space should look like:

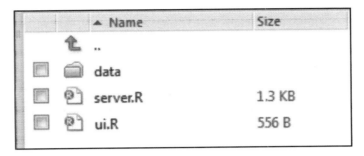

The ui.R file

Users interact with your app through the design in your `ui.R` file. The letters u and i are the abbreviation for **user interface** (UI). Be sure you have a directory called `Ch8-BasicShinyApp`. You will begin by creating an empty R script called `ui.R` and then adding the following code:

```
setwd("Ch8-BasicShinyApp")
library(shiny)
shinyUI(fluidPage(
    titlePanel("Revenue Prediction from Marketing Expenditures"),

    <<<Your design elements go here>>>
    ))
```

The `shiny` package needs to be loaded as it contains the functionality you will use. The `shinyUI()` function should be at the beginning of every `ui.R` file. It prepares everything inside the function to render properly and communicate with the server-side logic as required. The `fluidPage()` function enforces an app format that stretches or narrows elements relative to the size of the browser window to make it more adaptable on mobile devices with smaller screen widths. The `titlePanel()` function adds a title at the top of your app page. Finally, take a note of the location of the last two parentheses. Everything we added previously then wraps up additional elements that make up the UI of the application.

A world of widgets: The exciting part of designing a Shiny app is adding elements to the page that allow the user to interact with the R functionality. This interactivity is the main driver for moving away from static analysis reports and into Shiny apps. You have likely seen other web pages that use interactive elements such as radio buttons, drop-down lists, checkboxes, and text inputs. Shiny typically calls these input objects **widgets**. There are many different types of widgets, more than can be presented here. Learn about this world of widgets by visiting the following two resources for a complete listing of design solutions:
http://shiny.rstudio.com/gallery/widget-gallery.html
http://shiny.rstudio.com/tutorial/lesson3/

For your marketing expenditure app, you have decided to use a slider input widget to allow interactivity. The marketing expenditure slider will provide an input expenditure to predict an output revenue using your linear regression model.

The code for the slider input is straightforward. The function is called `sliderInput()`. In this example, the function takes the `inputId`, `label`, `min`, `max`, and `value` parameters. These define the characteristics of a slider widget placed in the Shiny app UI:

```
sliderInput(inputId="spend", label="Expenditure Level in $K:",
            min = 54, max = 481, value = 250)
```

The parameters used in this code are explained as follows:

- The `inputId` parameter is a reference for the value input by the user. A Shiny app might have multiple widgets on the same page and even more than one slider widget. For these reasons, `inputId` is the unique name `spend` to reference this particular widget.
- The `label` parameter can be any text you think is appropriate to inform the user about how to use the widget. In this example, the label informs the user that it establishes the marketing expenditures in thousands of dollars.
- The `min` parameter sets the floor of the allowed input. Your linear regression range (from your earlier work) began at 53.65. You will set the `min = 54` to keep the user input inside the linear regression range.
- The `max` parameter sets the high end of allowed input. Again, from previous experience, you know the maximum range of your model is `481`.
- The `value` parameter allows the Shiny app developer to set a default when the app opens. You will set it around the midpoint at a value of `250`.

Now, you will place the slider widget on the page. The `sidebarLayout()` function is a design theme that includes a `sidebarPanel()` area for widgets on the left-hand side of the page and a larger `mainPanel()` area on the right-hand side for output, such as the regression plot:

```
library(shiny)
shinyUI(fluidPage(
    titlePanel("Revenue Prediction from Marketing Expenditures"),
    sidebarLayout(
        sidebarPanel(
            sliderInput("spend", "Expenditure Level in $K:",
                        min = 54, max = 481, value = 250)
        ),
        mainPanel(
            plotOutput("prediction_plot")
        )
    )
))
```

The `plotOutput()` function tells the browser to render a plot from the output called `prediction_plot` that will flow in from the `server.R` file. This completes the code for the `ui.R` file. You have created a user interface in a Shiny app.

When the `server.R` file is complete, a visual of your Shiny app appears as follows. The `ui.R` file drives the slider input and overall design, and the `server.R` file drives the output plot. Notice that the user has selected an input of $250,000 for marketing expenditures. This results in a prediction of $44,990 in revenue with a range of $38,940 to $51,040 shown by the orange dashed-line prediction interval. All the results are calculated using the code you wrote in Chapter 4, *Linear Regression for Business*, but now it is a fully interactive app:

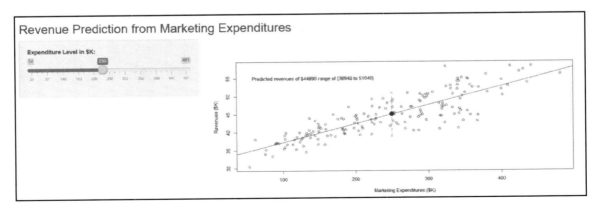

The variety and complexity of user interfaces that you can achieve are amazing. We encourage you to dream big about what you want to do. Then, systematically work through the application layout and experiment with widgets to achieve your design.

The server.R file

We mentioned that the `server.R` file contains the server-side logic and executes on the server hosting your Shiny app. Just like the UI that is initially defined by the `shinyUI()` function, the server is initially defined by the `shinyServer()` function. Create an empty file called `server.R` and add the `shinyServer()` function:

```
shinyServer(function(input, output, session) { ... })
```

You will code the majority of the logic inside this function, shown by the ellipses in the preceding code. The `input` and `output` parameters should always be included because the `input` parameter pulls all the user input actions from the UI side and the `output` parameter pushes all the server-side data and plots back to the UI. The third parameter, `session`, is not required, but is encouraged in certain cases as it allows you to define specific variables for each user session. Remember, more than one person might use your Shiny app at the same time, and by creating session-specific variables, this experience can be made unique to each user as they can interact simultaneously with the app.

Now, we said that the majority of code in `server.R` will be inside the `shinyServer()` function. An exception is logic that will only need to be run once when the application launches. For these cases, it is encouraged to place this code above and outside the `shinyServer()` function. This changes the scope of variables, which is an advanced topic that we will cover in more detail later in this chapter.

In this simple app, you only need to read the dataset and fit the regression model one time, so its logic will be above and outside of the `shinyServer()` function:

```
library(shiny)
revenue <- read.csv("./data/Ch8_marketing.csv")
model <- lm(revenues ~ marketing_total, data = revenue)
```

The following is the code that makes up the remaining parts of the `server.R` file. We will explain this code that is broken down into five chunks of logic performed by the app, as follows:

```
shinyServer(function(input, output) {
    output$prediction_plot <- renderPlot({
        plot(revenue$marketing_total, revenue$revenues,
            xlab = "Marketing Expenditures ($K)",
```

```
            ylab = "Revenues ($K)")
    abline(model, col = "blue")
    newdata <- data.frame(marketing_total = input$spend)
    pred <- predict.lm(model, newdata, interval = "predict")
    points(c(rep(input$spend, 2)), c(pred[2], pred[3]),
           pch = "-", cex = 2, col = "orange")
    segments(input$spend, pred[2], input$spend, pred[3],
             col = "orange", lty = 2, lwd = 2)
    points(input$spend, pred[1], pch = 19, col = "blue",
           cex = 2)
    text(54, 55, pos = 4, cex = 1.0,
         paste0("Predicted revenues of $",
                round(pred[1], 2) * 1000,
                " range of {", round(pred[2], 2) * 1000,
                " to ", round(pred[3], 2) * 1000, "}"))
    })
  })
```

The following is an explanation of the previous code:

- The server logic is initiated by `shinyServer(function(input, output) {...})` so that it can receive the slider input value coming from the UI and send the rendered plot back.
- The `output$prediction_plot <- renderPlot({...})` line of the code contains the `renderPlot{}` function. It will wrap any R plot so that you can pass it as the output variable back to the UI for the user to view. All outputs back to the UI will follow the `output${name}` naming convention. Look back at the main panel in the `ui.R` file. It expects an output object called `prediction_plot` to the `plotOutput()` function.
- The third logic chunk consists of the `plot()` and `abline()` functions that create a scatter plot of the data and a fitted line from the regression model.
- The fourth chunk is similar to work you did in linear regression, but with one Shiny element included: it depends on input from the UI. This chunk takes the `input$spend` slider input value to form a data frame called `newdata`. This input passes to the `predict.lm()` function to retrieve that prediction from our model. Notice how this slider input value is pulled from the UI using the `input$spend` variable. Refer back to the `ui.R` file and see that the `inputId` slider is `spend`. It passes to the `server.R` file and is identified on the server side by its `inputId`.
- The final chunk creates the accent points, line segments, and text to enhance and label the outputted plot. Once again, you will see the use of `input$spend`, which is used in this instance to specify the x-axis location in the `points()` and `segments()` functions.

Now you can run your Shiny app. Once you save the `ui.R` and `server.R` files, click on the `Run App` button in the right-hand top corner of the code script pane in RStudio. There is a drop-down list next to the **Run App** button where you can decide how the app opens on your computer via a separate window, within an RStudio pane, or externally in your default browser:

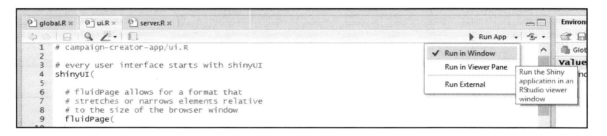

After clicking on `Run App`, you will see the application with your slider input and a regression plot. You can move the slider to the left and right and see that the predicted point and line segments move dynamically with your interactive input. The text at the top of the plot also changes with the input. The slider input responds to the mouse or arrow keys.

Reactive components: Shiny apps are interactive and use a specific strategy to function while the application is changing based on the user input. In order to respond to user input, Shiny uses a concept called reactivity. **Reactivity** means that the server-side logic waits for a user to perform an action on the UI before executing new calculations. Reactivity is even smart enough to know when the UI is different enough to invalidate the existing server state. This also performs new calculations. You can think of reactivity as a chain reaction to user input. If the user changes something that a server-side component depends on, then the server-side reacts to this change. Any other server-side components linked to changing components will also change and ripple through until they are complete.

The marketing expenditures app that you just created depends on reactivity in order to properly respond to user input. The plot depends on the user inputting a prediction value. For the app to respond to this user input, the server-side logic must have defined a reactive component that depends on the `input$spend` user input. In our case, the `input$spend` user input appeared inside the `renderPlot({ ... })` function, which is a reactive function. As described earlier, reactive functions recalculate whenever inputs inside them change. We placed the `input$spend` variable inside a reactive function and it causes a recalculation and rendering of the plot every time the user changes the slider input. This is the beauty of reactivity, it recalculates exactly when we expect it to and nothing more, so it is using server resources efficiently.

Learn more: The concept of reactivity can be difficult to understand without a complete review of examples. You can learn more about reactivity at `http://shiny.rstudio.com/articles/reactivity-overview.html`.

Creating a marketing-campaign Shiny app

The book has developed examples of analysis projects for Bike Sharing LLC. Now you will extend one of these by building a second Shiny App. In `Chapter 5`, *Data Mining with Cluster Analysis*, you spent time researching targeted customer marketing segments to help the marketing group identify clusters of customers and drive more effective marketing campaigns. Imagine that marketing wants the ability to interact with the analysis and explore differing numbers of clusters. They would also like to generate lists of customers who fit a particular profile so that they can act on potential campaigns more quickly.

The following examples provide a sense of developing a more realistic and useful Shiny app. The code snippets do not generate a complete web app, but rather focus on the added core functionality.

We highly recommend that you use the complete code for the marketing campaign app by navigating to the `Ch8-CampaignCreatorApp` repository folder. Follow along and find the snippets within the larger context of the project. Using this complete code also ensures the required packages install correctly. The code base is available on the book's website at `http://jgendron.github.io/com.packtpub.intro.r.bi/`.

One potential solution is building a Shiny app. A design might allow the marketing team to choose a clustering method (hierarchical or k-means), the number of clusters, and a downloadable list of potential customers based on their cluster membership. You can build this app using the same approach as our simple marketing expenditure to revenue predictor app by thinking through the user interface, and then building the server-side logic.

Using more sophisticated Shiny folder and file structures

RStudio will automatically create the `ui.R` and `server.R` files if you create a new project and choose **New Directory** and **Shiny Web Application** as the type. However, you will often want to create additional folders and files when designing more sophisticated Shiny apps.

The www folder

Most web applications contain extra resources or libraries to enhance their appearance and functionality. Shiny apps are no different. If you would like to include images, styling, or even JavaScript, then all of these files should be contained inside a single folder titled `www`, which is located in the same directory as the `ui.R` and `server.R` files. The `www` folder is the main location for all web resources in your application. If you would like to enforce a global standard of styling, then create a `.css` file containing a style sheet language for formatting.

Professional implementation: If you are deploying your Shiny apps in a professional setting, it is best practice to format and style your apps using rules defined by the CSS stylesheet language. This will reduce the amount of work to style new applications and provide a clean and consistent experience so that users quickly become familiar with how elements of your app function, based on their consistent appearance and functionality in other apps. Using CSS in Shiny apps is no different from styling a traditional web page, so any resource teaching CSS will help, such as the W3Schools CSS tutorial available at `http://www.w3schools.com/css/`. A Shiny CSS guide is also available at `http://shiny.rstudio.com/articles/css.html`.

If you want to add images or GIFs to your Shiny app, then place them in the www folder as well. Shiny supports most image file formats, such as .jpg, .png, and .gif. If you want to add JavaScript logic, create a .js file containing any functions or variables that you would like to execute. Again, place this file inside the www folder.

Learn more: Adding custom JavaScript to Shiny apps is an advanced user topic. Several Shiny packages allow you to leverage JavaScript without needing specialized knowledge. The shinyjs package does require JavaScript knowledge, but not as much as a web developer. If you have enough experience to write your own JavaScript, then you can learn more about how to embed it into Shiny apps. The following tutorial provides good information on this topic: https://ryouready.wordpress.com/213/11/2/sending-data-from-client-to-server-and-back-using-shiny/.

The www folder can contain multiple CSS files, image files, and JavaScript files. The idea is to keep all your web resources in this single folder so that you can keep track of what resources are available for the application in one location. However, it is important to realize that, just because a file exists in the www folder, it does not mean that Shiny loads the file. We will show an example of how you must explicitly source the file contents into the Shiny app in order to use these web resources.

The global.R file

It is good practice when coding software to place commonly used pieces of logic in a central location. You can put this concept into practice by creating a global.R file for each of your Shiny apps. The global.R file is not a requirement for a Shiny app, but it will reduce redundant code and increase the speed by reusing logic and variables from a global scope among concurrent app users.

The global.R file should be located in the same directory as the ui.R and server.R files. Whenever a Shiny app is first used, the global.R file makes its logic available to the ui.R and server.R files. This speeds up your app as it is only runs once. Typically, global.R is a good place for loading libraries, sourcing R functions or variables needed by your app, and setting options such as stringsAsFactors = FALSE.

Designing a user interface

The best Shiny apps are usually the result of thoughtful user interfaces. The purpose of creating a Shiny app is to share insights with a data consumer. Often, it can be a challenge to switch your thinking from the perspective of a data analyst to data consumer. We strongly recommend that you take out a pencil and paper to sketch out, or wireframe, what a fully functional Shiny app would look like before writing any code.

 BI tip: There are professions devoted to formulating habit-forming and visually impressive application designs. BI is the most useful when the user continually engages with the content. Enjoy this creative process and embrace it, or enlist the help of others at this stage. User experience is critical for the ultimate success of your Shiny app, so do not take this process lightly.

The head tag

HTML documents contain a head element identified by a `<head>` tag. The head tag identifies a portion of the web page, usually not visible to the user, that contains the application title, icon, metadata, and scripts.

In Shiny apps, the head tag is created using the `tags$head()` function. Inside the function, you can define the page title using `tags$title()`. If you have created CSS or JavaScript web resources in the `www` folder, they should be loaded in the head tag of the UI using the `tags$link()` function.

Here are some examples, but there is no need to type them into your console. Assume that you have an `app-styling.css` file inside the `www` folder that contains plain-text formatted in the CSS language. The following is how you could code that in the head tag:

```
tags$link(rel = "stylesheet", type = "text/css",
        href = "app-styling.css")
```

You can even add web bookmark icons in the head tag:

```
tags$link(rel = "shortcut icon", type = "image/x-icon",
        href = "bike-shortcut-icon.ico")
```

Adding a progress wheel

After defining the elements of the head tag, you can add the elements of the page that the user can view and use. One recommendation is to add a progress indicator in your Shiny app. Often, Shiny apps involve calculations that take more than one second to execute. It can be a frustrating experience for the user to interact with an application and wait without knowing what is happening. Is the application busy doing some calculation? Did the user select the correct button? Is the server down? You have likely been in this situation yourself.

A simple progress wheel can keep the user engaged. There are a few different ways to implement a progress indicator, but we have found the simplest and most effective solution in the `shinysky` package. The `busyIndicator()` function allows you to specify a custom message and wait time before the progress wheel appears:

```
busyIndicator(text = "Calculation in progress ... ", wait = 0)
```

Using a grid layout

Designing the layout of a web application page can be difficult. One challenge is aligning the elements containing information that you would like to convey. Fortunately, Shiny includes a grid-based layout framework based on the Bootstrap project to help you tackle this challenge.

 Learn more: If you have experience in web development, you may have used Bootstrap. It is helpful in standardizing the appearance of web pages. You can learn more about the Bootstrap project and what it can do at `http://getbootstrap.com/`.

There are two main functions in the Shiny implementation of the Bootstrap framework: `fluidRow()` and `column()`. These functions separate the page layout into rows of content that are fluid with the page width. These rows are further divided into columns to create a grid. The following chunk of code creates a row with a column element containing text. Again, there is no need to type this into your console:

```
fluidRow(
    class = "vertical-align",
    column(12, "Hello, this is my Shiny App")
)
```

In the previous example, you will notice that we assigned an HTML `class` attribute to the row. If a CSS file was loaded in the head tag and provided styling for any elements with a `class` attribute titled `vertical-align`, then the CSS styling will be applied to this row.

You might also notice that the number 12 appears as a parameter to the column() function. This number indicates how many units the particular columns should occupy in the entire row as one row might have many columns. We recommend creating a maximum of three columns per row, otherwise, the content will squeeze itself into a tight space.

Learn more: Columns utilize the Bootstrap 12-unit-wide grid system, so the total number of units in any given row is 12. You can learn more about Shiny app layouts at

`http://shiny.rstudio.com/articles/layout-guide.html`.

UI components of the marketing-campaign app

Here are some of the components of the marketing-campaign app broken down into implementation code to show you how to use and tailor Shiny widgets.

One design element will be a radio button to toggle between k-means and hierarchical clustering methods as options:

```
radioButtons("cluster_method", label = "Clustering Method?",
            choices = c("K-means", "Hierarchical"),
            selected = "K-means", inline = FALSE)
```

Another design element will be a second slider input that allows the user to select the number of clusters between a minimum of two and a maximum of ten:

```
sliderInput("cluster_count", label = "How Many Clusters?",
            min = 2, max = 10, value = 6, step = 1)
```

There should also be an area devoted to displaying a plot of the clusters created from the selected method and a table to summarize the average values in the dataset for the membership of each cluster. Finally, there should be an area to display a table of potential customers based on their cluster membership with a button to download the data into a spreadsheet for the marketing team to use:

```
fluidRow(
    column(7, plotOutput("cluster_viz", height = "500px")),
    column(5, h3("Cluster Summary Table"),
            DT::dataTableOutput("campaign_summary_table",
                                width = "100%"))
    ),
    fluidRow(
    column(12,
        downloadButton("downloadDataFromTable","Download Table Data"))
    )
    fluidRow(
```

```
column(12,
        DT::dataTableOutput("campaign_table", width = "100%"))
)
```

Learn more: This code uses DT:: to render the data table as there is an R package called DT (version 0.1.40 or later) specifically to make feature-rich data tables in Shiny apps. You can learn more about this useful package from their website at http://rstudio.github.io/DT/.

Designing the server-side logic

Every web application has a frontend, but the real work happens behind the scenes on the server side. Shiny brings the power of R for statistical analysis and machine learning to a well-designed UI residing on the user's web browser so they can benefit from the server-side logic.

Variable scope

While building the basic Shiny app to predict revenue, we mentioned the concept of variable scope. The fact that each user has a unique set of session variables is an example of scoping. Scoping is a term in computer programming that refers to the fact that certain variables will be visible or not to the code based on the methods used to create and assign them. It is important to understand that any variables created in the server.R file will have a global scope if assigned above and outside the shinyServer() function. **Global scope** means variables are shared across all concurrent user sessions.

For example, if you load a dataset prior to defining shinyServer(), then all users will have the same dataset available. However, if you change this shared dataset inside the shinyServer() wrapper, then it will unexpectedly change across all other user sessions, which would be confusing for users.

R tip: If your Shiny app pulls data from a database and then performs calculations, it is best practice to pull the data from the database using the code outside the shinyServer() function so that the database call is only performed once and all the concurrent users of the Shiny app can utilize the same dataset. If the app manipulates the dataset, then simply create a copy of the global dataset before modifying the dataset to avoid affecting other users.

For this reason, it is important to understand which variables have global scope and which should be specific to the user session as defined inside `shinyServer()` with a session argument.

 Learn more: The rules for scoping in a Shiny app apply to `ui.R`, `server.R`, `global.R`, and any variables created from these files. You can learn more from `http://shiny.rstudio.com/articles/scoping.html`.

Server components of the marketing-campaign app

After you design and code the core UI components of the marketing-campaign app, you can put your knowledge about scoping and reactivity to practice inside the `server.R` file. First, you know that you will want to load the dataset from a .csv file above and outside the `shinyServer()` environment to create a globally-scoped market data frame:

```
setwd("Ch8-CampaignCreatorApp")
market <- read.csv("./data/Ch8_global_market_data.csv")
shinyServer(function(input, output, session) {...
```

Next, we will create a reactive component that responds to the `cluster_method` and `cluster_count` inputs from the UI, builds a model, and assigns membership based on this user configuration:

```
clustered_dataset <- reactive({
    result_dat <- market
    if (input$cluster_method == "K-means") {
        kmeans_model <- kmeans(x = market[, c("age_scale",
                                              "inc_scale")],
                        centers = input$cluster_count)
        result_dat$cluster_id <- as.factor(kmeans_model$cluster)
    } else {
        hierarchical_model <-
            hclust(dist(market[, c("age_scale", "inc_scale")]),
                method = "ward.D2")
        result_dat$cluster_id <-
            as.factor(cutree(hierarchical_model,
                             input$cluster_count))
    }
    return(result_dat)
})
```

In this example, an if-else statement reads in the cluster method selected by the user in the UI. If the user selects `K-means`, then the Shiny app builds a k-means model. Otherwise, it creates a hierarchical clustering model. This logic works on the fact that the radio button can only be one of the two values.

Additionally, you will notice that the code copies the `market` data into a new data frame called `result_dat`. The `market` data is global among all user sessions as a global variable, so assigning cluster membership onto the original `market` variable would impact all user sessions and provide conflicting or confusing results to the end user. For this reason, we will create a separate dataset and then manipulate that copy.

The preceding code examples provide a sense of developing the server-side logic. The complete code for the marketing campaign app server-side logic is available to view in the `server.R` file located on the book's website at `http://jgendron.github.io/com.packtpub.intro.r.bi/`.

After linking all the UI elements with the server-side logic, we have a fully functional app for the marketing team to use. The following is a screenshot of the Shiny app:

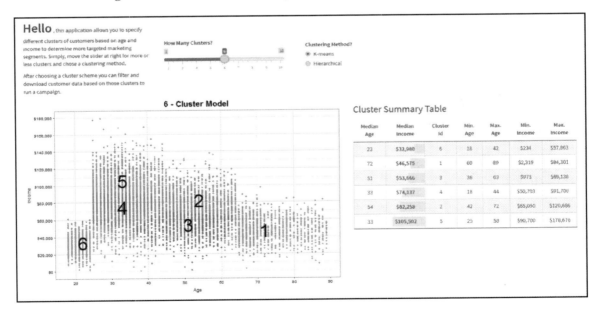

Deploying your Shiny app

Once you have created Shiny apps, you will want to share them with a broader audience. The following are three ways that are available to you:

- Located on GitHub
- Hosted on RStudio
- Hosted on a private web server

Each of these three options has its advantages and disadvantages based on your desired implementation, but you should typically find that one of the three suits your needs better than the others.

Located on GitHub

First, you might want to share with another R-savvy user. There are three options to run an app from a location online or a locally-cloned repository. For example, you can run the online version of the campaign creator Shiny app by opening R and running a code block pointing to its location on GitHub:

```
shiny::runGitHub(repo = "com.packtpub.intro.r.bi",
    username = "jgendron",
    subdir = "Chapter8-ShinyDashboards/Ch8-CampaignCreatorApp")
```

This method is extremely helpful when exploring various applications that others have created and you would like to explore the functionality yourself.

R tip: The runGitHub() function is just one of the three possible functions you can use to run a Shiny app from within RStudio. You can learn more at http://shiny.rstudio.com/reference/shiny/latest/runUrl.html.

Hosted on RStudio

If your audience does not consist of R users, then the app can be hosted online and accessible via the Web. This option requires a web server with special software installed to run Shiny apps, but there is a tool for people without access to such a server or permissions to install the software. The RStudio team has graciously provided a free hosting option. If you are using RStudio for developing the R code, then a small blue icon will appear in the right-hand top corner of the scripting panel whenever you are editing a `server.R` or `ui.R` file:

This will automatically wrap up your code, web resources folder, and other components and push them up to a web server hosted by RStudio. You will need to set up a free account before pushing your app for hosting. Review the details and terms on their website at `https://www.shinyapps.io/`.

Commercial-scale apps: The server software needed to host Shiny apps queues operations triggered by user inputs if another operation is running in the app. If your Shiny app will be used by a larger number of individuals at a given time, then consider structuring computationally-intensive operations in a way that minimizes wait time. You might also consider using **Shiny Server Pro** to host your Shiny apps on a commercial scale.

Hosted on a private web server

The alternative to having RStudio host your apps is to provision your own server and install **Shiny Server** (the software designed to run the Shiny apps on the server). These solutions require a higher level of expertise in systems and networking that cannot be covered here; however, more information is available at `http://shiny.rstudio.com/tutorial/lesson7/`.

Summary

Congratulations! You have taken important steps towards making your data analysis more accessible and engaging to a broader audience. Learning how to transfer your R code into a Shiny app will help others understand the power of your analytical prowess.

In this chapter, you learned how to break down the complex task of designing a business intelligence web application into a few key building blocks. The important first step is to recognize the difference between client-side and server-side logic, and how each is composed in the ui.R and server.R files. For the UI, you learned to sketch out a solution, review the widget gallery, and iterate through these two steps to design your user interface. From a server perspective, success comes from understanding reactivity and how each of the inputs should trigger a certain reactive component. You may find it helpful to map out the flow of server-side logic that takes the UI components and links them to reactive components and back to the UI so that you can visualize the round-trip that occurs when the user modifies the UI. There are many resources that will facilitate your understanding of Shiny. The RStudio tutorial is a great place to start:

http://shiny.rstudio.com/tutorial/

The book's journey has ended, but your journey as a business analyst in the R community has just begun. You first learned steps to get data and clean it. Then you learned four different analysis techniques to explore and create a model suiting your needs. Finally, you learned how to make your analysis actionable through visualization and web-based applications in Shiny.

> *"What is the next best skill to learn? Find and solve problems. In this process, you will continue to gain new and useful skills."*
>
> *– Jay Gendron*

Peace.

A
References

The following is a list of references used throughout the book, starting from the Preface and including the chapters:

Preface:

Guerra, P. & Borne, K. (2016, February). *Ten Signs of Data Science Maturity*. Sebastopol, CA: O'Reilly Media, Inc.

LawrenceStats. (2016, March 22). *RStudio Basics: Install & Load an R Package* [Video file]. Retrieved from `https://www.youtube.com/watch?v=H3EFjKngPr4`.

Peng, R. (2012a). *Setting Your Working Directory and Editing R Code (Mac)* [Video file]. Retrieved from `https://www.youtube.com/watch?v=8xT3hmJQskU`.

Peng, R. (2012b). *Setting Your Working Directory and Editing R Code (Windows)* [Video file]. Retrieved from `https://www.youtube.com/watch?v=XBcvH1BpIBo`.

Peng, R. (2014a). *Base Plotting part 1* [Video file]. Retrieved from `https://www.youtube.com/watch?v=AAXh0egb5WM`.

Peng, R. (2014b). *Base Plotting part 2* [Video file]. Retrieved from `https://www.youtube.com/watch?v=bhyb1gCeAVk`.

Peng, R. (2014c). *Control Structures in R (part 1)* [Video file]. Retrieved from `https://www.youtube.com/watch?v=8RmwEBo8yy0`.

Peng, R. (2014d). *Control Structures in R (part 2)* [Video file]. Retrieved from `https://www.youtube.com/watch?v=z8V-a6d8JTg`.

Peng, R. (2014e). *Data Types part 1* [Video file]. Retrieved from `https://www.youtube.com/watch?v=vGY5i_J2c-c`.

Peng, R. (2014f). Data Types part 2 [Video file]. Retrieved from
`https://www.youtube.com/watch?v=w8_XdYI3reU`.

Peng, R. (2014g). Data Types part 3 [Video file]. Retrieved from
`https://www.youtube.com/watch?v=NuY6jY4qE7I`.

Peng, R. (2014h). Installing RStudio [Video file]. Retrieved from
`https://youtu.be/bM7Sfz-LADM`.

Peng, R. (2014i). Subsetting Basics [Video file]. Retrieved from
`https://www.youtube.com/watch?v=VfZUZGUgHqg`.

Peng, R. (2014, April 9). Subsetting Matrices [Video file]. Retrieved from
`https://www.youtube.com/watch?v=FzjXesh9tRw`.

Peng, R. (2015a). Install R for Mac [Video file]. Retrieved from
`https://www.youtube.com/watch?v=uxuuWXU-7UQ`.

Peng, R. (2015b). Install R for Windows [Video file]. Retrieved from
`https://www.youtube.com/watch?v=Ohnk9hcxf9M`.

R Core Team. (2016, June 21). R: A Language and Environment for Statistical Computing. R
Foundation for Statistical Computing (Version 3.3.1) [Software]. Available from `https://ww
w.R-project.org/`.

Chapter 1 – Extract, Transform, and Load:

Cyberfella, LTD. (2013). Configuring an Excel ODBC Data Source in Windows 7 [Web log].
Retrieved from `http://www.cyberfella.co.uk/2012/06/11/windows7-odbc/`.

Kaggle. (2014, May 28). Bike Sharing Demand [Data file]. Retrieved from `https://www.kaggle
.com/c/bike-sharing-demand/data`.

Mulcahy, R. (2007, March 6). Business Intelligence Definition and Solutions [Web log]. Retrieved
from
`http://www.cio.com/article/2439504/business-intelligence/business-intelligence-
definition-and-solutions.html`.

Press, G. (2013, May 9). A Very Short History of Big Data [Web log]. Retrieved from `http://ww
w.forbes.com/sites/gilpress/213/5/9/a-very-short-history-of-big-data/#758da7
255da`.

RStudio. (2015, January). Data Wrangling with dplyr and tidyr Cheat Sheet. Retrieved from `http
s://www.rstudio.com/wp-content/uploads/215/2/data-wrangling-cheatsheet.pdf`.

Chapter 2 – Data Cleaning:

Gelman, A. & Hill, J. (2006). Data Analysis Using Regression and Multilevel/Hierarchical Models. New York, NY: Cambridge University Press.

Grolemund, G. & Wickham, H. (2011, April). Dates and Times Made Easy with lubridate. *Journal of Statistical Software, 40(3).* Retrieved from `https://www.jstatsoft.org/article/view/v040i03`.

Jonge, E. de & Loo, M. van der. (2013). Discussion Paper: An introduction to data cleaning with R. Retrieved from `https://cran.r-project.org/doc/contrib/de_Jonge+van_der_Loo-Introduction_to_data_cleaning_with_R.pdf`.

Levy, J. (2013). Bad Data Lurking in Plain Text. In McCallum, Q. E. (Ed.), *Bad Data Handbook* (pp. 53-68). Sebastopol, CA: O'Reilly Media, Inc.

Miller, G. A. (1956). The Magical Number Seven, Plus or Minus Two: Some Limits on Our Capacity for Processing Information. *Psychological Review, 63(2), 81-97.* doi:10.1037/h0043158.PMID 13310704.

Vries, A. de. (2015, June 24). How many packages are there really on CRAN? [Web log]. Retrieved from `http://blog.revolutionanalytics.com/215/6/how-many-packages-are-there-really-on-cran.html`.

Wickham, H. (2015, April 30). Introduction to stringr. Retrieved from `https://cran.r-project.org/web/packages/stringr/vignettes/stringr.html`.

Chapter 3 – Exploratory Data Analysis:

Anscombe, F. J. (1973). Graphs in Statistical Analysis. *American Statistician 27(1): 17-21.* Retrieved from `http://www.sjsu.edu/faculty/gerstman/StatPrimer/anscombe1973.pdf`.

Hoaglin, D. C., Mosteller, F., & Tukey, J. W. (1983). Understanding Robust and Exploratory Data Analysis. New York, NY: Wiley.

Johnson. (n.d.). Chapter 15: Descriptive Statistics. Retrieved from `http://www.southalabama.edu/coe/bset/johnson/lectures/lec15.htm`.

Kahn, S. (2016). Hypothesis testing and p-values [Web log]. Retrieved from `https://www.khanacademy.org/math/probability/statistics-inferential/hypothesis-testing/v/hypothesis-testing-and-p-values`.

Peng, R. D. (2015, September 3). Exploratory Data Analysis with R. Retrieved from `http://leanpub.com/exdata`.

Stat Trek (2016). What is Hypothesis Testing? [Web log]. Retrieved from `http://stattrek.co m/hypothesis-test/hypothesis-testing.aspx`.

Stevens, S. S. (1946, June 7). On the Theory of Scales of Measurement. *Science, 103*(2684), 677-680. doi:10.1126/science.103.2684.677.

Tukey, J. W. (1977, January 1). *Exploratory Data Analysis*. Reading, PA: Addison-Wesley.

Vigen, T. (2015). Correlation Chart [digital image]. Retrieved from `http://tylervigen.com/spurious-correlations`.

Wright, K. (2016, July 15). Examples for the corrgram package. Retrieved from `https://cran.r-project.org/web/packages/corrgram/vignettes/corrgram_examples.html`.

Chapter 4 – Linear Regression for Business:

Kahn, S. (2016). Hypothesis testing and p-values [Web log]. Retrieved from `https://www.khanacademy.org/math/probability/statistics-inferential/hypothesis-testing/v/hypothesis-testing-and-p-values`.

Rauser J. (2011, September). What is a Career in Big Data? [Video file]. Retrieved from `https://www.youtube.com/watch?v=tuEEnL61HM`.

Robinson, D. (2015, January 16). K-means clustering is not a free lunch [Web log]. Retrieved from `http://varianceexplained.org/r/kmeans-free-lunch/`.

Sicular, S., (2013, March 27). Gartner's Big Data Definition Consists of Three Parts, Not to Be Confused with Three "V"s [Web log]. Retrieved from `http://www.forbes.com/sites/gart nergroup/213/3/27/gartners-big-data-definition-consists-of-three-parts-not-t o-be-confused-with-three-vs/#b1728a43bf62`.

Stat Trek (2016). What is Hypothesis Testing? [Web log]. Retrieved from `http://stattrek.com/hypothesis-test/hypothesis-testing.aspx`.

StatSoft. (2016). How To Find Relationship Between Variables, Multiple Regression. Retrieved from `http://www.statsoft.com/textbook/multiple-regression`.

Chapter 5 – Data Mining with Cluster Analysis:

Berkley University. (2011, March 16). Cluster Analysis. Retrieved from `http://www.stat.berk eley.edu/~s133/Cluster2a.html`.

Han, J. (2011). Data Mining: Concepts and Techniques. Waltham, MA: Morgan Kaufmann Publishers.

Chapter 6 – Time Series Analysis:

Hyndman, R. J. (2016). Hyndsight [Web log]. Retrieved from
`http://robjhyndman.com/hyndsight/`.

The Pennsylvania State University. (2016). Welcome to STAT 510 – Applied Time Series Analysis.
Retrieved from `https://onlinecourses.science.psu.edu/stat510/node/33`.

Chapter 7 – Visualizing the Data's Story:

Bache, S. M. (2014, November). magrittr: Ceci n'est pas un pipe [Web log]. Retrieved from
`https://cran.r-project.org/web/packages/magrittr/vignettes/magrittr.html`.

Cairo, A. (2013). The Functional Art: An introduction to information graphics and visualization.
Berkeley, CA: New Riders.

Community NVD3 (2016, July). NVD3 documentation [Web log]. Retrieved from
`https://nvd3-community.github.io/nvd3/examples/documentation.html`.

*Eschelman-Haynes, C., Gendron, G. R., Hall, S., & Hall, B. (2016). Visualizing Big Data: Telling a
Better Story.* In *Proceedings from MODSIM World 2016.* Retrieved from
`http://www.modsimworld.org/papers/2016/Visualizing_Big_Data.pdf`.

Leaflet-Extras. (n.d.) Leaflet-providers preview. Retrieved from
`http://leaflet-extras.github.io/leaflet-providers/preview/`.

RStudio (2015, March). Data Visualization with ggplot2. Retrieved from
`http://www.rstudio.com/wp-content/uploads/2015/12/ggplot2-cheatsheet-2.0.pdf`.

Shneiderman, B. (1996). The Eyes Have It: A Task by Data Type Taxonomy for Information
Visualizations. *Proceedings of the IEEE Symposium on Visual Languages, 1996,* 336-343. doi:
10.1109/VL.1996.545307.

Vaidyanathan, R. Russell, K., & RStudio. (2015). htmlwidgets for R [Web log]. Retrieved from
`http://www.htmlwidgets.org/`.

Wickham, H. (2010). A Layered Grammar of Graphics. *Journal of Computational and Graphical
Statistics, 19*(1), 3-28. doi:10.1198/jcgs.2009.07098. Retrieved from `http://vita.had.co.nz/papers/layered-grammar.pdf`.

Wilkinson, L. (2005). The Grammar of Graphics (statistics and computing) (2nd ed.). New York:
Springer.

Chapter 8 – Web Dashboards with Shiny:

Allaire, J. (2014, January 24). Application layout guide [Web log]. Retrieved from `http://shiny.rstudio.com/articles/layout-guide.html`.

Bootstrap Project (n.d.). Bootstrap [Web log]. Retrieved from `http://getbootstrap.com/`.

Grolemund, G. & Cheng, J. (2014, May 6). Style your apps with CSS [Web log]. Retrieved from `http://shiny.rstudio.com/articles/css.html`.

Heckmann, M. (2013, November 20). Sending data from client to server and back using shiny [Web log]. Retrieved from `https://ryouready.wordpress.com/213/11/2/sending-data-from-client-to-server-and-back-using-shiny/`.

RStudio (n.d.-a). Add control widgets [Web log]. Retrieved from `http://shiny.rstudio.com/tutorial/lesson3/`.

RStudio (n.d.-b). DT: An R interface to the DataTables library [Web log]. Retrieved from `http://rstudio.github.io/DT/`.

RStudio (n.d.-c). Run a Shiny application from a URL [Web log]. Retrieved from `http://shiny.rstudio.com/reference/shiny/latest/runUrl.html`.

RStudio (n.d.-d). Share your apps [Web log]. Retrieved from `http://shiny.rstudio.com/tutorial/lesson7/`.

RStudio (n.d.-e). Shiny Widgets Gallery [Web log]. Retrieved from `http://shiny.rstudio.com/gallery/widget-gallery.html`.

RStudio (2014a). Reactivity: An overview [Web log]. Retrieved from `http://shiny.rstudio.com/articles/reactivity-overview.html`.

RStudio (2014b). Scoping rules for Shiny apps [Web log]. Retrieved from `http://shiny.rstudio.com/articles/scoping.html`.

RStudio (2016a). Share your Shiny Applications Online [Web log]. Retrieved from `https://www.shinyapps.io/`.
RStudio (2016b). Teach yourself Shiny [Web log]. Retrieved from `http://shiny.rstudio.com/tutorial/`.

W3Schools.com (n.d.). CSS Tutorial [Web log]. Retrieved from `http://www.w3schools.com/css/`.

B
Other Helpful R Functions

This appendix lists the chapter-wise R functions that will help us during our analysis.

Chapter 1 – Extract, Transform, and Load

The following table describes some helpful functions for `Chapter 1`, *Extract, Transform, and Load*:

Function	Description
`getwd()`	This returns the current working directory as a path in the R console
`setwd(<path>)`	This changes the working directory to `<path>` that you pass in the function
`dim()`	This returns the dimensions of an R object

Chapter 2 – Data Cleaning

The following table describes some other useful functions for `Chapter 2`, *Data Cleaning*:

Function	Description
`as.character();` `as.factor();as.logical()`	These are the functions to perform type conversion, such as `as.numeric()` seen in `Chapter 2`, *Data Cleaning*.
`class()`	This is used on an R object to determine the data type that the object is stored as.
`encoding()`	This reveals the encoding scheme that is used in storing the object.

`grepl();grep()`	These are the functions in the base R package that use regular expressions to find instances of a search string.
`gsub()`	This is the function in the base R package that allows for global substitution of a string with another.
`impute(x, fun = mean)`	This is a function to impute a vector of values based on the average of existing values. This is used with `x[is.na(x)]` to isolate missing values.
`install.packages()`	This downloads and installs packages that are not included in Base R from CRAN-like repositories.
`is.null()`	This finds NULL variables that are simply empty items in an observation.
`nrow();ncol()`	These are used to determine the number of rows or columns in a data frame.
`read.table()`	This is the underlying function of all other `read` functions. It is very flexible and is useful in tailoring how you read in data.
`readlines()`	This is useful for reading data that is raw text that is not in a tabular format.
`strsplit()`	This is useful when manipulating text data by splitting a string into substrings based on a separator value provided.

R Packages Used in the Book

The following table lists the packages used in the book by chapter:

Chapter	Package, in order of appearance
Chapter 1, *Extract, Transform, and Load*	RODBC, dplyr
Chapter 2, *Data Cleaning*	stringr, lubridate, and DataCombine
Chapter 3, *Exploratory Data Analysis*	psych, corrgram, and lubridate
Chapter 4, *Linear Regression for Business*	dplyr, MASS
Chapter 5, *Data Mining with Cluster Analysis*	dendextend, dplyr, and colorspace
Chapter 6, *Time Series Analysis*	TSA, forecast, dplyr, lubridate, and tbats
Chapter 7, *Visualizing the Data's Story*	ggplot2, scales, magrittr, leaflet, reshape2, and rCharts
Chapter 8, *Web Dashboards with Shiny*	devtools, shiny, shinysky, DT, dplyr, ggplot2, scales, dendextend, and RColorBrewer

In general, you will install R packages using the install.packages("{package name}") function from the console. For instance, to install the dplyr package, you will type the following in your R console:

```
install.packages("dplyr")
```

Most R packages are available at https://cran.r-project.org/web/packages/.

Two packages used in this book, rCharts and DT, are installed directly from GitHub. They are referenced in Chapter 7, *Visualizing the Data's Story*, and Chapter 8, *Web Dashboards with Shiny*, respectively. At the time of publication, the versions of these packages available on CRAN did not have the required functionality or could not be installed directly from CRAN in the typical way.

```
install.packages("devtools")
library(devtools)
install_github(repo = 'ramnathv/rCharts')
install_github(repo = 'rstudio/DT')
```

GitHub is a free code-hosting platform for better version control and collaboration. Authors of R packages will host new code on GitHub to encourage transparency and collaboration. This code is often actively being updated and changed, so they contain features and perhaps bugs that do not exist in a formal package release on CRAN. These *bleeding edge* package versions can be installed directly from GitHub using the devtools R package.

R Code for Supporting Market Segment Business Case Calculations

The code for supporting market segment business case calculations in Chapter 5, *Data Mining with Cluster Analysis,* is as follows:

```
# create dataframe with columns for distances

compare <- cbind(clus, dist2 = rep(0, dim(clus)[1]),
                dist3 = rep(0, dim(clus)[1]))

# -------
# functions to find distance based on Spherical Law of Cosines

distance2 <- function(lat, long, clus_id) {
    acos(sin(lat * pi / 180) * sin(two$centers[clus_id, 1]
        * pi / 180) + cos(lat * pi / 180) *
        cos(two$centers[clus_id, 1] * pi / 180) *
        cos(two$centers[clus_id, 2] * pi / 180 - long *
        pi / 180)) * 6371  #in km
}

distance3 <- function(lat, long, clus_id) {
    acos(sin(lat * pi / 180)*sin(three$centers[clus_id, 1]
        * pi / 180) + cos(lat * pi / 180) *
        cos(three$centers[clus_id, 1] * pi / 180) *
        cos(three$centers[clus_id, 2] * pi / 180 - long *
        pi / 180)) * 6371  #in km
}
```

```
# -------

for (e in 1:dim(compare[1])[1]) {
    compare[e, 5] <- distance2(compare[e, 1], compare[e, 2],
                              compare[e,3])
    compare[e, 6] <- distance3(compare[e, 1], compare[e, 2],
                              compare[e, 4])
}

if(!require("dplyr")) install.packages("dplyr")
suppressMessages(suppressWarnings(library(dplyr)))
compare <- cbind(compare, hybrid = rep(0, dim(compare)[1]))

for (e in 1:dim(compare[1])[1]) {
    compare[e, 7] <- distance3(compare[e, 1], compare[e, 2],
                              compare[e, 3])
}

compare <- mutate(compare, temp_increase = (hybrid - dist3))

# -------

par(mfrow = c(1, 3))
hist(compare[ ,5], ylim = c(0, 80), xlim = c(0, 8),
     col = "lightgray", xlab = "Dist (km)", main = "Two Kiosks")
abline(v = mean(compare[ ,5]), lty = "dashed")

hist(compare[ ,6], ylim = c(0, 80), xlim = c(0, 8),
     col = "lightgray", xlab = "Dist (km)",
     main = "Three Kiosks")
abline(v = mean(compare[ ,6]), lty = "dashed")

hist(compare[ ,7], ylim = c(0, 80), xlim = c(0, 8),
     col = "lightgray", xlab = "Dist (km)",
     main = "Two (Hybrid Solution)")
abline(v = mean(compare[ ,7]), lty = "dashed")
par(mfrow = c(1, 1))

summary(compare)   #to indicate max

hist(compare$temp_increase, breaks = 4, xlab = "Distance (km)",
     main = "Distance Increase: Building Two Kiosks at Future Locations",
     col = "gray")
bins <- as.data.frame(table(cut(compare$temp_increase,
                   breaks = c(-1:5))))
text(seq(-.5, 4.5, 1), 50, cex = 1.1, col = 'black', bins[ ,2])

increase <- filter(compare, temp_increase > 0)
```

```
increase <- increase[ ,-c(1:7)]

summary(increase)

text(2, 80, paste("Average increase:", round(mean(increase) *
    0.62137119, 2),"miles")) # .62 mi/km
```

 You can also find this code integrated with all the code for Chapter 5, *Data Mining with Cluster Analysis,* on the book's website at `http://jgendr on.github.io/com.packtpub.intro.r.bi/`.

Index